The Healing Ministry

Emily Gardiner Neal

THE HEALING MINISTRY

A Personal Journal

CROSSROAD · NEW YORK

1982

The Crossroad Publishing Company
575 Lexington Avenue, New York, N.Y. 10022

Printed in the United States of America

Library of Congress Catalog Card Number: 82-061163

ISBN: 0-8245-0517-4

Teach me, good Lord,
to serve Thee as Thou deservest;
to give and not to count the cost;
to fight and not to heed the wounds;
to toil and not to look for rest;
to labour and not to seek for a reward
save that of knowing that I do Thy will.
Amen
Saint Ignatius Loyola

Contents

Preface

A number of people familiar with my books on the healing ministry and my active work in this ministry have suggested that I write my autobiography. This I cannot do for two reasons: first, because it would seem to me presumptuous; and second, because my life did not begin with my physical birth, but only when I came to know Him in whom we live and move and have our being (Acts 17:28).

However, mindful of the desire many of my friends and readers have expressed for a "personal" book as well as another on the healing ministry, I attempt to combine both in this volume. As a journal, describing something of my life here at the convent, this book will also be a continuation of the most exciting venture any of us can undertake. It is an extension of that journey which has no end, and which began for me over twenty years ago: the journey of a pilgrim Christian.

Born and brought up in New York, attending Brearley School and studying from an early age to become a professional violinist, I was the only child of parents who were atheists.

After my marriage to an Annapolis graduate (which caused complications during Army-Navy football games as my father was a West Pointer!) and the birth of our two daughters, I gave up the violin and worked for some years as a magazine feature writer. Assigned by a national magazine to do an exposé of the healing ministry and simultaneously conceiving a book[1] which would accomplish the same purpose, I was converted to the faith through my research. Ever since, having "learned Christ" in this way, I have devoted my life to Him and to the furtherance of this ministry.

The healing ministry of the Church is founded firmly on Scrip-

ture. Many fail to realize that one-third of the Gospels is devoted
to our Lord's earthly ministry of healing. Many more are unfamiliar with the writings of the early Church Fathers on this subject,
and the history of the ancient Church when healing flourished.

The ministry is simple but not easy, for it is filled with tensions.
One of the greatest of these is the fact that we ask people to hold
expectant faith, at the same time realizing that everyone who prays
for healing is not healed at the precise moment or in the exact way
that he may wish.

On the other side of the coin is the danger that a faith-filled individual may be so certain of his healing here and now that he re-
fuses to face the possibility of death. It is a paradox that until we
can share the dichotomy expressed by Paul, "For me to live is
Christ, and to die is gain—I am hard-pressed between the two"
(Phil. 1:21, 23 RSV), until like him, we lose our fear of death, we
cannot fully live.

This week's mail again brought me a number of letters asking
the question I hear most frequently wherever I go: "Should I not
go to a healing service just once, then claim my healing and leave
the matter in the hands of God? Isn't it a lack of faith to continue
to pray for healing?"

We leave our healing as we leave all things, in the hands of God,
thanking Him that He is at work within us. However, we *continue*
to pray for the completion of our healing, just as each day we pray,
"Give us this day our daily bread." To continue to go to the
Source of all healing in persistent prayer is scriptural (Mk. 7:25;
Lk. 11:5; 18:1), and in no way denotes a lack of faith. Quite the
contrary. It is indisputably His will that we go to Him again and
again. And again and again we are replenished and refilled.

All Christians are in the process of becoming, and this involves a
lifelong spiritual journey. The healing ministry is only one of the
Church's ministries, but it is a peculiarly effective means by which
to engage in our pilgrimage.

God heals through prayer alone, but I cannot overemphasize
what I believe to be the importance of regularly attending healing
services. It is through such services that we come to know and to
believe that important as are the healing of our bodies and emotions, it is a closer relationship with Christ Jesus which is of *su-*

preme importance. It is through such services that we are enabled by the Holy Spirit to resolve the tensions and avert the dangers inherent in this ministry. It is through such services that we come to understand what *wholeness* is, and that someone flat on his back may be more "whole" than an Olympics athlete bursting with physical health alone. It is through such services that we uniquely encounter the living Christ and are enabled, by grace, to receive more and more of Him as the door of our heart gradually opens wider and wider. It is through such services that we grow in the knowledge and love of God, which is a never-ending process. It is through such services that we come to experience and then reflect the love of God who is Himself, Love.

We who work in the healing ministry have to contend continually with the misconception that it is "magic." It is far from that, for its basic premise is: "Seek ye *first* the kingdom of God." While it is true that some are healed who have little or no faith and seem to flout every spiritual law we know anything about, the vast majority of us must follow certain spiritual disciplines. To be sure, this was not necessary in the time of our Lord: He saw a need and He met it. However, in today's world, and as none of us is Jesus Christ, we do well to follow a path which will facilitate our healing. This involves a discipline which is neither more nor less than that required of any sincere, practicing Christian, for the healing ministry is not "out there"; it is an inherent part of the faith.

This ministry is at once a subjective ministry and one of the most powerful means of intercession God has placed in our hands. It is in no way confined to physical healing, but includes the healing of all brokenness in every area of our lives. "I came that they might have life and have it to the full," Jesus says (Jn. 10:10). The abundant life He came to bring us cannot be restricted to our bodies, for we are not merely bodies; nor can it be confined to our spirits, for we are not solely spirit. He stretches forth His hand to heal every level of our beings: physical, mental, emotional, spiritual. The life abundant means wholeness, fullness of life in every aspect of our personhood. Further, in the healing ministry, we pray not only for the healing of individuals, but for all brokenness everywhere: for the pain, the suffering, the sin of our nation and the world. There is no limit to the scope of this ministry.

The Episcopal Church is considered by many to be "stuffy," and Episcopalians are often referred to (and not always facetiously!) as "God's frozen people," yet it is the Episcopal Church which from the beginning, has taken the lead in today's revival of the Church's ancient ministry of healing. At the present time, virtually every branch of the Church has within it at least some churches which practice healing. This is in part due to the fact that in 1961 a Healing Commission was appointed by the national Episcopal Church, to study in depth the ministry of healing. The Commission consisted of three bishops, three priests, two physicians, and one lay person, myself.[2] Our report, a treatise on the theology of healing, was submitted to the 1964 General Convention (the ruling body of the Episcopal Church in the United States).

This report was unanimously adopted by the Convention, and so much interest was generated by it that hundreds of extra copies were printed. A substantial number of these was passed on to clergy of other denominations at their request. Many of these ministers have said to me, "I figured that if the *Episcopal* Church issued such a report, the healing ministry must be sound!"

In general, both clergy and lay people who participate in the established Church's ministry of healing tend to be conservative. For this reason, I have pursued in this book the same policy I have followed in all my books, namely, I have juggled the cases of healing mentioned. This is to say, that while each episode recorded has occurred under the exact circumstances I have described, not every one has occurred during the specific mission to which I have ascribed it.

Last night, driving over to the weekly healing service at Saint Thomas Church, I was thinking of the homily I would soon be giving. Suddenly I realized that I had not mentioned the word "healing." (I might say that this is not an infrequent occurrence.) As soon as I arrived at the church, I took out my notes and inserted the word "healing" where appropriate. This was not difficult to do. Salvation and healing are the same word in Greek: the entire Gospel is a healing Gospel, and the healing ministry is the Gospel in action. This is why it is so exciting a ministry.

As we stand back and watch the Great Physician at work, as we see lives transformed and those in Christ become new creatures before our very eyes, we, like those two thousand years ago, are filled with awe and give praise to God (Lk. 5:26). We, like those two thousand years ago who were once blind, now see—and like them, we go on our way glorifying God.

"What we have seen and heard, we proclaim in turn to you" (1 Jn. 1:3).

The Healing Ministry

1.

Speak, Lord.
What Shall I Do?

January 6
The Epiphany of Our Lord

T he alarm clock jolted me awake. In the pitch dark I groped sleepily to turn it off. Glancing at the illuminated dial of the clock, I saw that it read four-thirty. Why on earth had it gone off at that hour? I must have set it incorrectly. And then I remembered: I was no longer in Pittsburgh where I had lived for so many years, but in an apartment situated on the grounds of the Convent of the Transfiguration, an Episcopal religious community where I had moved some months before. Sleepiness forgotten, my heart soared with joy, and once again my prayers of praise and thanksgiving rose, as incense, to God (Rev. 5:8). He had brought my life full circle in a totally unforeseen way.

Although Lauds (the communal morning office) followed by mass was not until six-thirty, I set the alarm so early in order to get in the best prayer time of the day, before activity took over. On this particular morning, however, memories of the not-too-distant past rushed in upon me and would not be stemmed.

I remembered how a few years after the death of my husband I believed I had a vocation to the religious life, and had made an appointment with a Mother Superior for an interview in late June. It was during the early part of that month that I injured my back. As a result, I found myself in late June, not in the Mother Superior's office but in a West Virginia hospital. The injury was serious, and my dream of becoming a religious would remain just that, a dream.

In the beginning I was heartbroken, but over the months and years ahead, I realized that I had mistaken the will of God. How could this be, I wondered, when I had prayed so hard and long and been so sure? Was it, perhaps, that I had confused His will with my own desire? (I have learned by now how easy this is to do, and how continually we must guard against this pitfall as we seek His will in our lives.) Or was it perhaps that my motive in wanting the religious life was wrong? The healing missions I had begun to lead all over the country were heady business. I was increasingly concerned lest people were placing their faith in *me* instead of in God. Convinced as I have long been that one thing which God will not tolerate is lack of humility, I was frightened—frightened that I might begin to see myself the way too many saw me. I felt that I would be protected by the anonymity of the religious life, protected from myself and the danger of spiritual pride. To surrender my entire life to Jesus, yes, I wanted this. But I wanted to select the way which I believed would be easiest for *me*. Or was it, perhaps, that what was being required of me was my *willingness* to enter the religious life?

These were questions I asked myself for a long time. As the missions multiplied in number, as more books were written, and I was engaged by the rector of Calvary Episcopal Church in Pittsburgh to lead weekly healing services and counsel at the church, I received my answer. I came to understand that it was all these things, and not the conventual life, which were the primary will of God for me, and I rejoiced to know that I was in His will. The Lord was to protect me from the danger of self-aggrandizement through His Church. Working always under her authority, firmly anchored in the sacraments, it was the Church which perpetually reminded me to whom I belonged, whom I strived to serve, and under whose lordship I lived and labored.

As I increased in knowledge and the missions grew in power, I came to realize that no one can feel anything except awe as he stands in the presence of almighty God, experiencing Him who pities and loves His children, observing the Great Physician of bodies and souls blessing and healing as the Holy Spirit pours Himself out, guiding, instructing, healing, and sanctifying His people. As the healing ministry became my life, so did it become an all-pervasive desire to fulfill the words of Micah: "To do right and to love goodness, and to walk humbly with your God" (Mic. 6:8).

However, throughout the years, I never lost my love for and interest in the religious life. I came to know well a number of religious communities, both Roman Catholic and Anglican, and, as frequently as time allowed, had visited them and was often privileged to pray for and counsel their sisters.

It was during a mission in Ohio that I first met Sister Virginia of the Community of the Transfiguration. She and I became close friends, and through her I was introduced to this community which I quickly came to love. I spent occasional weekends here, and remember saying more than once to Sister Virginia, half seriously and half in jest, "Couldn't I hide a mobile home on the convent grounds, and make my headquarters here?"

During the last two years in Pittsburgh I had a strong premonition that a drastic change was to occur in my life. I seemed to become increasingly aware that Christians are a pilgrim people, the Lord preceding us by a column of cloud by day and a column of fire by night (Ex. 13:21). Where, I wondered, was He going to lead me?

I was to find out one Monday morning, when I received the letter which was to change my life. It was from Sister Virginia and it said that an apartment on the convent grounds was soon to become vacant. Would I be interested in it?

I was stunned: first, because even after years of association with the community, I had no idea such a thing would be possible; and second, now that I was confronted with the real possibility of leaving Pittsburgh, I was far from sure that I wanted to go.

I prayed about the matter in a rather perfunctory way, decided that it was the will of God that I remain where I was and where I felt needed, and promptly dismissed the idea of the convent from my mind. A few months later during Lent, I had a speaking engagement near Cincinnati, and made plans to spend the weekend at the convent. Fifteen minutes before time to leave for the airport to fly home, I heard myself say to Sister Virginia, "Oh, that apartment you wrote me about, is it vacant now?" She nodded and I said, "Just out of curiosity, may I see it?"

I found the "apartment" was, in fact, half a cottage with its own front and back doors, located about two hundred yards from the convent. We walked in and I looked quickly around. More out of curiosity than interest, I asked, "Where is the kitchen?" The reply: "There isn't any"—followed by: "Arrangements could be made for you to have your meals at the convent." That was clearly impossible, with my irregular work schedule and thus totally irregular meal times.

My second question, asked with some embarrassment, as Sister Virginia must think me blind: "The closets, where are the linen and the clothes closets?" I was shown a tiny closet in the little hallway which might conceivably hold three coats and nothing else. But it was nice to have *any* kind of coat closet, I thought to myself. "The other closets?" I asked "There aren't any," she said.

I silently thanked God that *this* time I had not mistaken the guidance of the Spirit when I felt I should remain in Pittsburgh. Half a house with neither kitchen nor closets—and far too small—was manifestly impossible for me to live in.

"Thank you, Sister Virginia, I couldn't live here." Sister, having spent an occasional night with me in Pittsburgh on her way home from Philadelphia, readily agreed that it was not "up to my standard of living." We left for the airport without more ado.

The first thing I did when I got home was to make a cup of tea, with a new appreciation of a kitchen stove. Then I hung up my clothes, gloating over my spacious closets. I even peeked in my linen closet. I had never realized before now how thankful I should be for all those closets!

My thankful complacency was not to last long. The very next day I began to receive "nudges." I woke up wondering, "Could it *somehow* be possible?" But walking into the kitchen to make coffee, I glanced into my recently redecorated living room—at last just the way I wanted it—and said to myself, "Oh, no. And besides I'm needed here."

That night on the way to Calvary for the healing service, I found myself thinking, "Perhaps I could get *most* of my furniture into that little place, and most of my books. And couldn't I make a hot plate do?"

By then I was at the church, and my mind filled with what was at hand. However, the thought of that little half-cottage would not let me rest. Three days later I awoke, thinking, "Closets. . . . What about old-fashioned wardrobes? And how about an empty book-case with a curtain hung in front of it? Would that do for a linen closet?"

The Lord never ceased His "nudging," and I finally wrote Sister Virginia, asking her to let me know before they disposed of what was euphemistically called the "apartment." Even as I wrote, I was asking myself, "Why am I doing this when I know perfectly well I couldn't live under such conditions?"

Thus began four months of travail—of intensive and sometimes desperate prayer—in an effort to discern God's will. Whether or not to leave Pittsburgh was an agonizing decision. Now I can only wonder at the anguish involved and why I thought it made such a difference! However, at the time it did, for not only was it burning my bridges behind me, leaving my beloved Bishop Appleyard and the clergy of whom I was also very fond, but most of all, it was leaving "my" people. For so long I had sought to bring them, through Christ, healing and the joy of the Lord. How could I now bring them grief? I could not, unless I were absolutely sure it was God's will that I move. It was an emotion-fraught situation.

For weeks, the more I prayed the more confused I seemed to become. I had a key to my parish church, and many were the nights when, very late, I would let myself into the quiet church, the darkness pierced only by the sanctuary candle. I spent whole nights in prayer before the tabernacle, and learned a little of what it meant to "sweat drops of blood" (Lk. 22:44) as I pled, "Speak, Lord, for your servant is listening" (1 Sam. 3:9). Night after night my plea seemed to be met by a great silence.

I vacillated for weeks, feeling as if I were on a spiritual seesaw. One day I would be convinced that it was not God's will that I leave "my" people at Calvary who counted on me, and many of whom had supported the healing ministry for the entire ten years I had been there. The next day I would be equally convinced that it was His will that I go to new territory, meeting new challenges in His name and for His sake.

Reluctant to discuss the matter with my bishop until I had reached some conclusion, the time came when I could delay no longer. He was leaving shortly on a three-month sabbatical and I could not risk his returning from the Holy Land to find me gone without a word. A few days before his departure I told him what I was considering. His reaction was swift and vehement: "Don't go," and he offered me a variety of good reasons why I should stay where I was. I left his office convinced of my proper course. I had always tried to be obedient to his wishes, and I now accepted his response as the will of God, and was vastly relieved to have the matter settled. Only it wasn't, I couldn't get the convent out of my mind.

Three nights later, still mulling over the matter and unable to sleep, I got up and went to my reading chair. I sat for a moment, and the words went through my mind: "Your ways, O Lord, make known to me" (Ps. 25:4). Idly I picked up a small book resting on top of the pile by my chair. Not looking at the title, I flipped unthinkingly through the pages. My eyes were caught and held, by the words: "The first method of making a wise and good choice." I realized then that I had picked up a copy of *The Spiritual Exercises of St. Ignatius.* I continued to read. "I must have as my aim that end for which I am created, which is the praise of God our Lord and the salvation of my soul. I must be ready to follow the course which I feel is more for the glory and praise of God our Lord and the salvation of my soul."[1]

Yes, I knew all this, I thought impatiently. But which course *is* more for His glory?

I read on. "I must remain indifferent and free from any inordinate attachment." I thought hard over this sentence. Was I, perhaps, inordinately attached to my own diocese, to my security in Pittsburgh? And so many of "my" people who seemed to need me, were they not ready now to go out on their own, as knowledgeable and mature Christians?

My eyes went back to the book. "Acting upon the stronger judgment of reason and not on any inclination of the senses, I must come to a decision in the matter that I am considering." With that, I picked up a piece of paper and a pencil, drew a line down the center and painstakingly noted the advantages of leaving Pittsburgh in one column and the disadvantages in the other. Then I prayed as if for the first time, "Speak, Lord, your servant *is* listening." Suddenly there came so vivid an impression that I am still not sure that I did not actually hear the words: "The Lord, your God, is with you, wherever you go [Jos. 1:9]. Follow me and it shall be better than any known way."

At long last I had the answer. At mass next morning, the Host was accompanied by a blinding light, that light which dispels all darkness. This was the seal. As soon as I got home, I telephoned Sister Virginia and told her I would come.

With a start I looked at the clock: five-thirty. We are all familiar with the adage that one's entire life is relived the minute before drowning. I wasn't drowning, but now I tended to believe this myth. I had done a lot of reliving in only an hour. I only wished there were more time.

After Mass

Tonight is the monthly healing service in the convent chapel, and I still have the meditation to prepare. But it isn't difficult to speak about the healing Christ on Epiphany, which is the Church's feast day in commemoration of the coming of the magi, the first manifestation of our Lord to the gentiles. I always think of the healing ministry as the "Epiphany ministry," for it is one of the means by which He reveals Himself, with stunning clarity, to the peoples of the earth. It uniquely shows forth the love and power of Jesus. It is the Gospel in action.

2.

Your Servant Hears. I Go.

The healing service the other night was truly blessed. Sister Virginia played the magnificent new organ and her radiant joy touched everyone present. Between the new organ and the monthly healing services which she has for so long wanted, her cup of happiness is full. So is mine, for in the beginning many of the sisters were wary of the ministry of healing, but now a goodly number are coming to the services.

I love the beautiful Gothic chapel, and whenever there, feel I am indeed standing on holy ground. I thought throughout the service of the inestimable privilege of proclaiming the good news of "the unfathomable riches of Christ" (Eph. 3:8). To make known the riches of His glory (Rom. 9:23) is the great purpose of the healing ministry, and another reason I think of it as the "Epiphany ministry," for of course Epiphany is not just one feast day, but a season which extends until Lent begins: a season which celebrates the shining forth of the light of salvation to the whole world. It is a season of getting to know Jesus better and to love Him more, and this is what the healing ministry is all about.

As I awoke this morning, I remembered the woman who just last week had asked, "Why did Jesus have to be baptized if He were God?" Yes, fully God but also fully man. Jesus gives us the answer in His reply to the same question asked of Him by John the Baptist: "We must do this if we would fulfill all of God's demands" (Mt. 3:15). It was directly after His baptism that the sky opened and the Spirit of God descended upon Him and the Voice spoke, saying, "This is my beloved Son. My favor rests on him" (Mt. 3:17).

It was bitterly cold walking to mass, the sky leaden with an occasional snowflake drifting down, presaging the heavy snow which is forecast. It had been just such a day the first time I saw this apartment and said with conviction, "I can't possibly live here." Yet now as I sit in the attractive, cheerful living room, looking out the ice-etched windows which frame the branches of a great tree still glistening white from the last snowfall, I think not of that other winter day but rather of that Tuesday in June, when armed with tape measure, pencil, and pad, I walked into the newly painted half-cottage, the sun streaming in through sparkling bright windows. As I looked around that day, a great joy surged up in me as I inwardly exclaimed, "This is home. This is where I belong."

I gazed with something close to rapture at the small but complete kitchen the convent had installed for me, while to my delighted surprise I discovered that the living room measurements were far larger than I had remembered. Puzzled, I thought, "Lord, you have increased its size." But why not? He multiplied the loaves and fishes, didn't He?

That was the day I first met the chaplain of the community, an extraordinarily fine priest. There was instant rapport between us and it was clear that we were on the same spiritual wavelength. He was interested in the healing ministry, had read all my books, and was unabashedly enthusiastic about my coming here to live. He knew I had worked with both Episcopal and Roman Catholic religious, and envisioned for us a team ministry of counselling. After lunch that day, we attended a meeting of the community council where my work at the convent was officially spelled out: one day a week of counselling, and one healing service each month.

Just one more thing remained to be settled before I could make the move. I felt I must have some work in a parish church, doing what I had done at Calvary. The procurement of such work was the final "laying down of the fleece" (Jg. 6:39).

This I mentioned to the chaplain as he drove me to the airport that night. He promised to get in touch immediately with the bishop of the diocese of Southern Ohio. Within three days I had a telephone call from the rector of Saint Thomas Episcopal Church, nearly twenty-five miles from the convent, but easily accessible by expressway. I went back to Cincinnati the following week, to be interviewed by the rector and the vestry, and all was settled.

Planning to leave Pittsburgh in August, my next major decision was when to tell "my" people at Calvary that I was leaving. As I always left on vacation August 1, it seemed to me that the best time, that calculated to cause the least pain, would be at the last healing service in July. However, among "my" people were some who were severely disturbed emotionally and mentally. I called the psychiatrist of each one of these to check the wisdom of my decision, fearful that a sudden shock might prove harmful. They were in one accord that the way and the time I had chosen would be the least upsetting.

I was greatly touched by what most of these psychiatrists said in slightly different words: "Wherever you go, Mrs. Neal, I wish you well, and hope that the psychiatrists in Cincinnati will learn what many of us have come to know, that working in conjunction with you has been of enormous benefit to our clients. In fact," said several, "I told my client that if seeing both you and me each week proved too time-consuming for him, that he would be better off seeing *you* each week, and me only once a month." Surely a superlatively generous statement from medical men, the majority of whom were not Christians.

The psychiatrists with whom I had contact in Pittsburgh acknowledged the success of what I term the "three-pronged" approach for the emotionally disturbed, namely, psychotherapy, pastoral counselling, and regular attendance at healing services.

One of the most valuable lessons I learned during my training in pastoral counselling was to discern when one of my counselees needed more specialized help than I was qualified to give. In such cases, I would send my client for therapy either to a psychiatrist or a psychologist, whichever seemed appropriate. With the counselee's permission, his therapist and I would keep in occasional contact. I wanted to do nothing which would conflict with the psychotherapist's treatment. Between the therapist who dealt skillfully with the disturbed emotions and minds of some of "my" people, I who dealt with their spiritual lives as counsellor, and the Lord Jesus who dealt with the total person—body, mind, emotions, and spirit—at the regular healing services, there was an extremely high rate of healing.

One example of this approach, is a woman who had been under psychiatric treatment for years and who was declared to be without hope of rehabilitation. In a state of acute clinical depression, she came to me as a last resort. Desperate and almost totally nonfunctional, she presented the typical picture of acute depression: confusion, impaired memory, and virtual inability to summon up the energy necessary to get out of bed, let alone prepare a meal at home. Her husband and friends continually told the poor soul to "buck up," a too-frequent admonition by those who do not understand the suffering or acknowledge the symptoms involved in depression. Because they cannot see the ailment with their eyes, they cannot realize that it is an illness. To say "buck up" in such a case is like telling a skier with two fractured legs to "stand up."

I arranged with this woman to see a psychiatrist I chose, and asked her to come to me for weekly counselling and attend the healing services. On her third visit I was forced to call her psychiatrist and tell him that I was taking her, right then, to a psychiatric hospital as she was dangerously suicidal. She was hospitalized for two weeks, then returned to me. Her progress from that time on was steadily upward. One glorious night at Calvary healing service, many months after she had first come to me, she received, as usual, the laying on of hands. But this time she arose from her knees at the altar rail, the joy of the Lord on her face. "Praise God, I've been healed," she exclaimed. And she was.

This happened years ago and we are still in touch. She has had no recurrence of depression. This was a woman "without hope of rehabilitation" who is now leading a full and creative life. A psychiatrist alone could not have healed her. Her past history was ample proof of this. As a pastoral counsellor I could not have helped her, as her "up-tightness" impeded the inflow of the heal-

ing power of God. It was the three-pronged approach, of psycho-
and spiritual therapy plus the direct power of the healing Christ
which she was finally able to receive at the service of healing,
which was effective in rehabilitating her. She became, as have so
many, a new creature in Christ (2 Cor. 5:17).

As long as I live, I shall remember the farewell service at Calvary. For months afterwards, I dreamt of the stricken faces of
"my" people on that last night and would wake up crying.

I had told the priest participating in the service with me that
night what was going to happen, so he would be prepared. I had
thought *I* was, but it proved to be a situation comparable to a
death. When it occurs, no matter how one may be intellectually
prepared, one is never emotionally ready. And so it was with me
on that hot July night.

The homily was a recap of what seem to me the most salient
truths of the healing ministry, with the admonition never to forget
them as long as they lived. And then I told them. A look of
shocked disbelief fleeted across their faces, and then, silently, the
tears began to flow. When they came up to receive the laying on of
hands, they came quietly, all, men and women alike, in tears.

Every single person who came to the altar rail offered the same
prayer, not for themselves, but for me and for my welfare, offering
thanksgiving to God that they had had me for so long at Calvary.
These were my spiritual children I was leaving, and I was proud
that they had learned so well what I had been teaching them for so
long: "Offer thanksgiving to God for all He has given every one of
you and it doesn't matter what your state or condition. Thank
Him that He is God and loves you, and that you know it." But as
well as being proud, my heart was broken by their gallantry and
generosity of spirit. I was strongly tempted at one point to stop the
service and say, "Wait. I didn't mean it. It was just a bad joke." Of
course I didn't, just mingled my tears with theirs.

I left a part of my heart at Calvary, but I was soon to learn that I
had not left "my" people but simply gathered up more. The rector
and the people at Saint Thomas gave me a heartfelt and movingly

warm welcome. These are also "my" people, manifesting the love of God and sharing their lives with me.

The love of God is uniquely demonstrated in the healing ministry, that love which is at once Himself, His power to heal, and the tie that binds together those who gather in His name. All who come to Saint Thomas to the healing services for the first time remark on the love they experience there. This, of course, is the love of God from whom all love derives, as manifested through the people of God.

Healing services are also an example of ecumenism at work. At Calvary, at Saint Thomas, on mission, people from every branch of the Church are represented. These groups are representative of the Church Universal wherein resides the total power of the risen Christ.

If my welcome at Saint Thomas was warm, so was that extended to me by the Sisters of the Transfiguration. By their love they have made me one of their own, and I am deeply grateful.

Much as I love the chapel where Evensong and Sunday mass are sung, I also love the modern oratory within the convent where daily mass and the offices are said. (We will soon move the healing services to the oratory which is smaller, more intimate, and more convenient for the sisters.)

Like most religious communities today, this one observes four of the monastic offices daily. Each one of these consists largely of portions of the Psalms which the Church has always considered its most important book of prayer. These were the prayers of the prophets, the prayers of Jesus, and in this knowledge, they seem to bring Him very close. In short, the Psalms are the Church at prayer. It is through them, as Thomas Merton says, that "We drink praise at its pure and stainless source."[1]

The early morning office of Lauds is, to me, the most beautiful of all the hours. It is an hour of praise and preparation for the day which lies ahead. Following closely the church year, the climax of Lauds is invariably the Benedictus, the Song of Zechariah, that great hymn in praise of our redemption: "Blessed be the Lord God of Israel, for he has visited and redeemed his people" (Lk. 1:68–79 RSV).

Compline, the last prayer before sleep, is more subjective than the other offices. It is a prayer for the soul who makes her peace with God, a prayer for protection from the power of darkness, a prayer for all souls, everywhere.

Three times each day, morning, noon, and night, the Angelus is said in commemoration of the Incarnation of our Lord. "The Angel of the Lord announced unto Mary, and she conceived by the Holy Spirit."

The chapel bell rings out each noon for the Angelus. It is good to have a reminder in the middle of the day, to stop briefly to pray.

My Lord, I love you and thank you for bringing me here.

When I am on mission, people often ask, "Why did you leave Pittsburgh where you had it made?" Others say, "How can you bear to start all over again?"

To the first question, my answer invariably is: Perhaps just because I *did* have it made there. Then it was time to move on, both for "my" people and for myself—the "column of cloud," the "column of fire."

The answer to the second question: Although in one sense it has been to "start all over again," in another, it is simply a continuum of my life as lived for years. Obviously, the answer to both questions and the overriding reason for the move lies in the fact that it was without question the will of Him who sent me.

My bishop may have urged me to remain in Pittsburgh, but he has kept me in balance since. I think of one Sunday night the first winter I was here when I dreamt I was at Calvary laying hands on all "my" people. The next evening during the healing service at Saint Thomas the faces of the Calvary people kept floating before my eyes. For a few moments I had the eerie feeling of not knowing where I was. When I reached home that night, I was devastatingly homesick for Pittsburgh. Glancing at my watch, I saw that it was still early enough to call my bishop. I picked up the phone, dialed his number, and he answered. My first words were, "You were right, I never should have left." Firm and clear came his reply, "Yes, you should! You're exactly where God wants you."

Actually I knew this, but I needed to be told. In my heart I had known from the beginning that I could not and would not offer to the Lord my God that which cost me nothing (2 Sam. 24:24).

In the working out of His will, God had invited me to share a tiny bit in His passion and death. Now I have tasted the glory of the Resurrection.

It is late and tomorrow morning I leave at six o'clock to go on mission. Better get packed.

3.

The Healing Power of God at Work

January 18
Confession of Saint Peter

Returning from mission several days ago, I am at last caught up on the mountain of correspondence which invariably greets me when I have been away.

In one of the letters awaiting me this time, the writer says, "I don't think we should be awestruck when we receive a healing from God. We should just *expect* it." Expect it we certainly should, but throughout Scripture we are told to marvel at the mighty works of God. In this area at least, I will admit my total obedience: I am still as awestruck at every mission as I was at my very first, now years ago. The one just completed is no exception.

Thinking I was going to the far outposts of civilization, I was unprepared to find myself, after a torturously long trip, in one of the most beautiful churches I have ever seen. Like most of us I don't like to see vast sums of money poured into church buildings, but I never want to see the doors of such handsome churches closed. I remember well how a Roman Catholic missionary priest summed up this dilemma when his Church was under criticism for building costly edifices in poverty-stricken areas. "The church," he said, "is the only beauty these people have in their lives. When we tried to close our church because of the cost of upkeep, the people pled with us to keep it open."

I can well understand this. Man does not live by bread alone. As I worshipped and led the mission in this glorious church, I know how those people felt. I have much beauty in my life, thank God, but my soul was fed by the sheer glory of this house of the Lord.

The recently completed mission was unique in the ready acquiescence to my request to report healings which were occurring, so that the faith of others might be quickened. Frequently I am not told of healings until I happen to return to the same area perhaps five years later. At this time, people come up by the score, saying, "When you were here five years ago, I received the most marvelous healing of such and such." I have long since come to terms with this (although in the beginning it caused much frustration), seeing my task as merely to love and to obey. However, it is extremely helpful to those attending a mission to *know* what is going on.

Among the healings reported to me, was that of a lovely young girl, her beauty marred only by eyeglasses so thick that the lenses distorted her eyes. As she walked out of the church after the first healing service, she took off her glasses, handed them to me, and leaning forward, took a prayer book from the rack of the last pew. Opening it at random, she read the fine print without difficulty.

Then there was a man who had been driven two hundred miles to the mission by his Methodist pastor. He had glaucoma and was virtually blind. At the altar rail he instantly received his sight. (Time and again we note how God honors the active faith of those who make a great effort to come to a healing service.)

A woman long deaf received her hearing. A broken relationship between father and son was healed, as was the broken marriage of a clergyman and his wife who had travelled hundreds of miles to get to the mission.

Claiming His promise to heal the brokenhearted (Is. 61:1), a recently bereaved widow experienced His healing touch. She still grieved, which was right and proper, but now only for herself. The joy she felt that her husband was with Him whom he greatly loved transcended her own grief. Having met her Lord at the altar rail in a new way, this woman expressed guilt that she still grieved at all. When I reminded her that Jesus had wept at the death of Lazarus (Jn. 11:35), she smiled and departed in peace.

A man on crutches who could not even stand without their support, let alone walk, came to every session of the mission. By Friday night, the last healing service, the sense of expectancy in the church was palpable. As he struggled up to the altar rail, his face was incredibly radiant, not merely with expectant faith, but glowing with what seemed an inner knowledge. "Your presence, O Lord, I seek" (Ps. 27:8). One felt he was standing in it then.

As the five participating clergy remarked later, the extraordinary radiance of his countenance drew their eyes, as it had mine. One of the clergy expressed well what we all felt: "When I saw that man's face, I wanted to kneel." The man received the healing rite, walked on his crutches halfway back to his pew at the rear of the church, then stopped. Carefully removing first one crutch then the other from under his arms, he handed them to an usher and proceeded to walk alone the rest of the way.

An hour later when he said goodnight, I placed my hands on his shoulders, and there in the narthex of the church, we offered together our prayers of thanksgiving.

A curious phenomenon occurred midway during the mission as I was giving the evening meditation. I had been speaking about ten minutes when I began to lose my voice. I knew I had not overstrained it, and could not imagine what was happening. I drank some water but this was of no help, and within moments I found myself voiceless. At the precise moment that I opened my mouth and no sound came out, I became conscious of something evil, something definitely not of God, coming from somewhere in the congregation. I looked around quickly and my eyes focused on a group of people sitting in a front pew directly under the pulpit. Even as I looked, emanations of evil seemed to pour out from that particular pew. I prayed hard and drank some more water. I could feel the prayers of the people, and then an inrushing of power. My voice was back to normal. This whole episode probably lasted only about sixty seconds, although it seemed forever.

The bishop of the diocese was participating in the service that night. At its conclusion, he stepped up to the altar to give the blessing. He began in his usual strong voice: "The peace of God which passes all understanding keep your hearts and minds in the knowledge and love of God." When he came to the next words, "and of his Son Jesus Christ our Lord," his voice began to fade. When he came to the final words, "and the blessing of God Almighty, the Father," his voice went completely. In a whisper he concluded: "the Son, and the Holy Spirit be amongst you, and remain with you always."

The moment the bishop's voice began to falter, I saw a parallel between what was happening to him and what had happened to me. I prayed desperately hard. As the bishop, the clergy, and I left the sanctuary together, I was aware of a tremendous outpouring of the Holy Spirit. Then I did something I have never done before in my life at the end of a service: I faced the congregation and said in loud tones, "Thanks be to God who gives us the victory through our Lord Jesus Christ" (1 Cor. 15:57).

The rector of the mission church and I, not having eaten before the service, went out together for a late supper. As we talked, my curiosity got the better of me, and I said, "Do you by chance know who was sitting in the front pew directly under the pulpit? They seemed to be in a group." He thought for a moment and then replied, "Oh, yes. I guess you mean that group of spiritualists. They practice healing through mediums contacting the dead."

This, then, was the answer. Spiritualism is in total conflict with the Christian faith. This was why the bishop and I had lost our voices. Whether or not the spiritualists were intentionally working against us who preached the Gospel of Christ, I cannot know, nor does it matter. What *does* matter is that God does indeed give us the victory through our Lord Jesus Christ.

We are aware of the correlation between body and spirit. It was dramatically illustrated by the case of a woman suffering real agony from pain in one of her knees, which was grossly swollen and badly inflamed. She stood at the altar rail at the opening healing service obviously unable to kneel. After the service she asked if I would see her for a few minutes the following day. I agreed, and as we talked the next morning, I found her filled with a bitter hatred and deep resentment against her parents. I explained that the healing she needed most was not that of her knee but of her spirit, and that until she was liberated from her destructive emotions, there was no use praying for her knee.

That night she came to my section of the altar rail, and I prayed only that she might know the love of God, that by His grace she might be freed from her sins of the spirit. I thought she might be angry; many are if their physical ailments are not directly prayed for. To her great credit she was not, but rather was she joyful as she said she felt she had been healed of what mattered most: her resentment. At the final healing service she again was on my side of the church. As she had twice before, she stood to receive the laying on of hands, her face reflecting the pain she was enduring. The healing prayer was offered, this time for the knee, and preceded a thanksgiving that she had already received a spiritual healing.

In the middle of the prayer, she knelt; and at the end, arose to her feet with no difficulty. As we said goodnight and goodbye later, tears of joy streamed down her face as she pointed to her knee. There was no evidence of swelling or inflammation, and she said that she was completely free of pain. Again, we offered our thanksgiving in the narthex. This time others gathered around and joined in. Then, one by one, each offered a personal prayer in gratitude for the mission and the mercy of God so abundantly manifested, each praising God and thanking Him for the blessing and healing he or she had received. It was a moving experience.

The rector drove me to the airport next morning. We arrived early enough to stop in the restaurant for a cup of coffee. It was there that he spoke the words which sent me home in total joy. "I have never in my ministry seen God so glorified as in this mission." Then he added, "Only God came through at this mission. Emily Neal was completely hidden in Christ." That meant more to me than anything else.

All the way home my heart sang the Sanctus: "Holy, holy, holy Lord, God of power and might, heaven and earth are full of your glory. Hosanna in the highest."

Today we celebrate the Confession of Saint Peter, with whom, in so many ways, I can closely identify. Often I say to Jesus in the same spirit as did Peter, "Lord, no matter what happens, I'll never deny you" (Mt. 26:35). Yet Peter *did* deny his Lord, and I think to myself, "Under the same circumstances, would I have denied

Him, too?" Alas, very probably, for I realize that in a slightly different way, I inadvertently deny Him now, to the exact extent that I deny His teaching. How? In many different ways. Too often, for example, I fail to forgive as quickly or completely as I should. "Of *course* I forgive you," I say—and then, to myself, "but it's going to take me a long time to really forget this episode." *This* is not forgiveness at all. We aren't forgiving unless at the same time, we have forgotten.

Sometimes I am too impatient. Sometimes I fail to love the unloveable with the sort of love commanded by our Lord. When I realize what I am doing or failing to do, I remember Peter, and like him, I "go out and weep bitterly" (Mt. 26:75).

But then, suddenly, I remember something else and my heart soars. Jesus *knew* the tremendous love of Peter for Him, just as He knows mine, regardless of my failures. I remember how Jesus said, "You are Peter, and on this rock I will build my church, and the powers of death shall not prevail against it. I will give you the keys of the kingdom of heaven" (Mt. 16:18–19 RSV).

Obviously He did not build His Church upon any of us today, but He gave us all a set of the keys to the kingdom when He gave us, and continues to give us, Himself.

In His third post-Resurrection appearance, Jesus says to Peter, "Simon, son of John, do you love me more than these?" and Peter replies, "Yes, Lord, you know that I love you." Then Jesus says, "Feed my lambs" (Jn. 21:15). As Peter denied our Lord three times, so does he answer the question put to him three times: "Do you love me?" "Yes, Lord." "Then feed my lambs." Jesus ends his discourse by saying to Peter, "Follow me" (Jn. 21:19).

These words apply to all Christians today, both clergy and laity. We are all to feed the lambs who come our way, by telling them of the love of God. And in all that we do, we are to follow Him to the best of our ability, always empowered by His grace which is unfailingly given. To be sure, we stumble and fall along the way, but His hand is outstretched to help us up again, and in the distance we glimpse that light which is Himself, always beckoning us onward.

Following Him is what we are trying to do in the healing ministry of His Church. "Heal the sick," He said and still says, and this is precisely what the healing Church is doing today in His name, by the power of the Holy Spirit.

It was breathtakingly beautiful coming home from mass this morning. On my left the sky suffused with the rose and gold of the dawn, on my right the full moon, both seen through a veil of softly drifting snow. "I lift up my eyes," not to the hills but to the heavens, knowing well from whence comes my help and the help of the world.

Time now to get to work on the meditation for the Saint Thomas healing service.

4.

Road to the Kingdom

Paul on the road to Damascus—the sudden flash of light—and he falls to the ground. Then the Voice: "Saul, Saul, why do you persecute me?" Saul's question: "Who are you, sir?"; and the answer: "I am Jesus, the one you are persecuting" (Acts 9:4-5).

The conversion of Paul, who from that day on would devote his entire life to Jesus, who would become the great apostle to the gentiles, the one who knew best the mind of Christ and would write, "I have been crucified with Christ, and the life I live now is not my own; Christ is living in me. I still live my human life, but it is a life of faith in the Son of God, who loved me and gave himself for me" (Gal. 2:19-20).

I think of this on today's feast day, and of the times without number I have seen people brought to Christ through the healing ministry as they come face to face with the living God. Sometimes it is a Damascus road experience, but more often it is a slow, growing process through which the heart gradually opens so that one is able to receive more and more of that which He stands ready and eager to give: Himself. Then, as a bonus if you will, we come to realize that "My God will supply your needs fully, in a way worthy of his magnificent riches in Christ Jesus" (Phil. 4:19). One of my own greatest blessings has been the discovery that when we know Jesus, those things which used to seem all-important now fade into insignificance. Like Paul, we "come to rate all as loss in the light of the surpassing knowledge of my Lord Jesus Christ" (Phil. 3:8).

Looking out the window, I see a few snowflakes lazily drifting down, and my mind reverts again to the last mission. I remember the discussion time when someone stated, "I'm a Christian, I keep the ten commandments." So many are under the impression that this is all the Christian faith requires. Obviously the ten commandments must be kept, but the mere keeping of them does not make any one of us a Christian.

Our Lord summarized them when He said, "You shall love the Lord your God with your whole heart, with your whole soul, and with all your mind. This is the greatest and first commandment. The second is like it: You shall love your neighbor as yourself. On these two commandments the whole law is based" (Mt. 22:38–40).

St. Augustine tells us to "love and do what you will." These words have been woefully abused. The word "love" has been prostituted into sloppy sentimentality in whose name we can commit every sin in the book. However, we know how Augustine meant his statement, namely, if we truly love God all the elements of the faith will fall into place, and all those factors inherent in the faith will be practised.

If we love God, we will repent of our sins, because to sin hurts Him whom we love. If we love God, we will grow in grace and knowledge of Him, for the more we love Him the more we desire Him, long to know Him better. If we love Him, we will strive to follow Him and to obey His commandments, because we long to be holy as He whom we love calls us to be holy.

I remember too, at this same mission, how a gentleman made the assertion that the golden rule is Christianity in action. With this statement I have to quarrel. The same thing obtains as with the ten commandments: a good Christian must certainly follow the golden rule, but the mere following of it does not necessarily make one a good Christian.

"Treat others the way you would have them treat you" (Mt. 7:12) is by no means a uniquely Christian precept. Not only does it predate Christianity, but it is a part of all the world's great religions. Thus, although it is a command from Jesus and, as such, to be followed, it did not originate with Him. In my experience, today's usage of the term "golden rule" seems, frequently, to exchange the inherent truth of an ethical concept for a self-serving principle: "If I do this favor for you, then you'll have to return it by doing a favor for me." Again and again I have seen this bargaining technique used even in our prayers. It does not work. We cannot bargain with God. And if, in the name of the golden rule, we do someone a favor and at the same time expect a return, we are not following the law of love.

The gentleman at the mission who brought up the subject came to see me for three brief counselling sessions. He was in trouble both emotionally and physically, suffering from hypertension, recurring chest pains, and most painful of all for him, depression.

The constant reiteration of "I live by the golden rule" made me suspicious during our first session together. In our second session my suspicion was confirmed. His story exemplified the danger of making the golden rule the be-all and the end-all of the Christian faith.

The man was a junior executive in a large corporation. His immediate superior was a heavy drinker and consequently incompetent. In a loyal effort to protect his boss from *his* superior in the company's hierarchy, my counselee carefully corrected every piece of work the man submitted. On more than one occasion, he even lied for him, saying that he had become ill with a migraine headache and had to go home when, in fact, the "headache" was too many martinis for lunch.

In due course my counselee had gotten into some trouble. It was a small thing, but instead of trying to cover for him, his immediate superior reported him, exaggerating the error out of all proportion to the mistake made. The result: my counselee was soundly castigated by the higher-up. He was extremely bitter over this, feeling that the episode threatened his promotion. Said he, "And after all I've done for *him!* I'll never forgive that man!"

A natural, human reaction. But the Christian faith demands more of us than a so-called "human" reaction. "Love your enemies," Jesus says, and what could be less "natural" than that!

All the time my counselee was talking, he kept alluding to the golden rule. He simply did not realize that this is never intended to be a means of bargaining, but rather, according to the teaching of

Jesus, the law of love in action, and love demands nothing in return, not even love.

I tried to explain that outside the context of the Gospel, the golden rule can be, and often is, simply a self-serving axiom. It is only within the Gospel context that it becomes infinitely more than a rule of conduct. It demands real love from those who follow it.

I also pointed out that resentment against his co-worker was actually making *him* sick. Working eight hours a day beside a man he detested, he was under continual stress and strain, and the not unexpected physical result could well be hypertension and chest pains caused by tension. This seemed to me almost certainly true in this case where there was no history of hypertension prior to the trouble at work.

During our three counselling sessions we made considerable progress. I explained the absolute necessity of ridding himself by God's grace of his antagonism toward his co-worker; of holding him up three times daily in the light of God's love, with the prayer, "Please, Lord, forgive me for being unable to love Ralph just now. Please help me to love him. Meanwhile, please love him for me." I also suggested that he pray for the healing of Ralph's drinking problem.

Yesterday I received a letter from him and the news is good. He still cannot really like Ralph, but now he can pray for him wishing him only good, and he is praying for the healing of his own resentment. His blood pressure is down fifteen points and he has no chest pains.

I have never known this method of prayer to fail if persisted in for a sufficiently long time. It may be that we shall never come to *like* the person we hold up in the love of God, but liking is not of primary importance although it is a welcome dividend. Even Jesus had His "beloved" disciple (Jn. 20:2). However, by grace, we can *love* in Christ to such an extent that we are ready to lay down our life, if necessary, for the one we cannot "like."

As Christians we turn to Jesus who spoke to *us* when He said, "Treat others the way you would have them treat you" (Mt. 7:12). We seek His help that a rule which expresses an ethical code may be transformed into that principle of love which our Lord intended. He was the founder of a faith, not an ethical code, and He said, "If a man wishes to come after me, he must deny his very self, take up his cross and begin to follow in my footsteps" (Mt. 16:24).

Christianity is not mere intellectual assent or the observance of certain rules. It is the following of a certain Person, and with a flaming faith. The important thing is that we know the value of a personal experience of Christ, however it may come about, for without it we dare not call ourselves Christians and upon it depends our wholeness, our very life.

Someone whom I am counselling regularly but infrequently as he lives far from Cincinnati said to me last time I saw him, "All my life I've been a nominal Christian. I want to know Jesus, but I'm discouraged. I don't even know what it is to 'experience' Christ."

This is nothing to be ashamed of. The real danger lies in not acknowledging this truth to ourselves.

There are a number of things that those who are hungry to experience God may do. The first thing is to acknowledge, as did this man, that we do *not know* Him, even though we may know all *about* Him. A genuine surrender on our parts is a necessity if we would experience Christ, and this is not easy. There must be a determination to die daily to self, to *decrease* so that He may *increase*, to be willing to give all for His sake: those material things to which we are inordinately attached, our associations, desires, ideas, ambitions, our doubts and fears and sins. It is in the giving of all these things which, in essence, constitute ourselves that He makes Himself known to us, in different ways to different people.

Our quest for the knowledge and love of God; our *desire* to obey unfalteringly, for we inevitably falter; our gradually increasing sensitivity to the leading of the Spirit—all these comprise an ongoing, never-ending process. Love, faith, obedience, self-abandonment to God—these are the flagstones which pave the way to the kingdom. It is neither a smooth nor an easy road to traverse. He never said it would be. But it is the most exciting and wonderful road in the world.

The healing ministry has to a great extent recaptured the dynamism and the passion of the faith. However, this ministry, as is true of every aspect of the faith, is a costly thing. The rewards are beyond description and without price. Nevertheless, the cost, especially of the healing ministry, cannot be denied. That is why this ministry will never become a truly "popular" ministry within the Church. For this we can probably rejoice as we remember how Christianity became a nominal, largely lip-service religion when popularized by Constantine.

Where does the cost lie? It lies in involvement. All of us associated with the healing ministry in any way become deeply involved with those who suffer, and not with them only but with a suffering world.

It lies in obedience. To obey in order to receive His blessings is a hopeless proposition. We can never be close to Him unless we obey simply because we love. How can we love Him more? Never by ourselves, but as St. Paul tells us, by the Holy Spirit: "the love of God poured out in our hearts through the Holy Spirit who has been given to us" (Rom. 5:5).

Above, beyond, and undergirding all else, the cost is love: loving God, loving one another, loving the unloveable, and in so doing, becoming, ourselves, vulnerable. "To say love is to say sacrifice," says Karl Rahner. The only way we can be sure whether or not we love someone is to ask ourselves whether we are willing to pay the price of love. It is high. It can be the cross.

Are we willing to pay it? Yes, because as Christians we know that by the cross comes resurrection.

"I have been grasped by Christ Jesus," says St. Paul. Thank you, Lord, that I have also, and that now I can never turn back nor will I want to. I remember your words, "Whoever puts his hand to the plow but keeps looking back is not fit for the reign of God" (Lk. 9:62).

Throughout the Gospels our Lord makes abundantly clear that there is a higher loyalty than any in the world: Himself. Am I willing to give first priority to following Him, to give Him the only priority in my life? Am I willing to lose my life for His sake? Yes, Lord, and I have dared to claim your promise and you have, in your mercy, fulfilled it: to him who loves the Lord do you manifest yourself (Jn. 14:21).

Those lazy snowflakes I saw earlier today have multiplied themselves into a blinding storm. With diabolical regularity it seems to snow every Monday, reaching blizzard-like proportions around seven o'clock in the evening when I leave the house for the twenty-three mile drive to Saint Thomas for the weekly healing service. Tonight is no exception. As I pull on my boots, I wonder if anyone will venture out on a night like this, except me!

5.

Inner Healing

Bad as the weather was last night, we had a respectable number of the faithful at Saint Thomas, undeterred by the storm. As always when getting to a healing service involves great difficulty, it seemed to me that God blessed our efforts by an unusually abundant outpouring of the Spirit. Nearly everyone in the church seemed to share my awareness, for as they said goodnight, virtually all commented on their almost startling experience of the presence of Christ. He was certainly beside me as I slithered home over the icy road, blinded by the snow which, whipped by gales of wind, was hurled against the windshield forming an almost impenetrable solid white curtain. Never have I been so thankful to reach the convent gate!

It must have snowed all night, for when I turned on the outside light and looked out this morning, all I could see was what appeared to be mountains of snow. I opened the back door with some trepidation, but as usual, Lawrence and his maintenance crew had cleared off my steps and shovelled a path to the convent. Thank God for Lawrence and his co-workers without whom I could not live!

Last week one of my counselees told me that she had been a Christian all her life and believed she had a close relationship with God. "But," she said, "every time I hear a 'born-again' Christian witness, I somehow feel inferior."

I remember that remark today as we honor Paul's companions, the evangelists Timothy and Titus. Especially do I think of Timothy, whose commitment to our Lord was not due to a Damascus road conversion like St. Paul's, for Timothy had been born and raised in a Christian family (2 Tim. 1:5). While it is true that the faith of his parents or grandparents could not save *him*, it gave him a good start.

The same holds true of us today. Regardless of the faith of our forebears, each of us must make his or her own personal commitment to Christ. However, to grow gradually in grace and in the knowledge of God implies no less a "born-again" experience than a sudden conversion. The commonly used phrase today, "born again," is incorrect and unscriptural, since *all* Christians, no matter how they come to the faith, must be, as Jesus tells us, "begotten from above" (Jn. 3:7). This is implicit in the sacrament of Holy Baptism, when we become in Him a new creation. If we are baptized as infants, it remains for us to appropriate our baptism. In doing this, we are born again, for as Jesus says, "No one can enter into God's kingdom without being begotten of water and the Spirit" (Jn. 3:5). In the waters of baptism we are buried with Christ in His death; by baptism we share in His resurrection; through baptism we are born again by the Holy Spirit (1 Pet. 1:3–2:10).

There is great emphasis today on inner healing: the healing of the memories. This is not a new method of prayer; Agnes Sanford wrote of it many years ago. However, the fact that it is being emphasized today has resulted perhaps in an increased sense of expectancy. Hence there are more such healings than ever before and often dramatic ones. Since there are some excellent books on this subject alone, I give here only the briefest summary of this type of prayer.[1] It consists of asking Jesus to go back in time in the life of the disturbed person, requesting that He heal the trauma of each phase of his or her life. Some degree of pastoral counselling (and frequently some psychotherapy) is ordinarily a concomitant to the prayer for inner healing. However, over the past several years I have noted a significant number of either instantaneous or very rapid healings when neither I nor anyone else has had any prior knowledge of the person involved. In addition to the usual advisability of counselling as an adjunct, the prayer for inner healing is so long as generally not to be possible at a public healing service. However, on more than one occasion, a person has travelled a great distance for one service and this specific prayer, and is unable to return.

I recall, for example, one woman who came up to the altar rail in a very agitated state and asked prayer for the healing of memories. I had never seen her before, and I explained that this prayer was too lengthy to pray under the circumstances. However, when she told me tearfully that she had flown into Cincinnati that day expressly to attend the service, and was flying home at midnight, I asked her to wait until the others had been ministered to, and then I would take her alone. This we did, I praying that the Holy Spirit would pray in me, making intercession according to the will of God, as I did not know how to pray (Rom. 8:26–27).

At the end of the prayer, she arose from her knees, radiant, her countenance replete with that peace of God which does indeed pass all understanding. I knew she had been healed, and together we thanked God.

She was extremely grateful to me, although obviously I had had nothing to do with the matter. As she left the church, she asked what she could do for me to express her gratitude. My request was twofold: first, I asked her to let me hear from her. She readily agreed and for two years has written regularly. Now that she has told me her full story, her instantaneous healing seems specially remarkable. She has also commented that the prayer led by the Spirit touched on those very areas of trauma in need of healing. (This did not seem in the least remarkable to me!) My second request was that every night before she went to sleep, she would pray, "Into your hands, Lord, I commend my spirit, and ask you to heal, while I sleep, everything within me which has need of healing." This, too, she has continued to do. It is an ideal way, incidentally, for any of us to drop off to sleep. I pray this prayer regularly for myself.

Most physicians concur that the fetus can be influenced by the attitude of the mother carrying the baby. Time and again I have had the validity of this theory confirmed in my own experience, which is why, when praying for the healing of memories, I go back not only to the person's childhood but to the time when the individual was *in utero*.

The importance of this first became apparent to me when, within a fairly brief period of time, a number of adoptive parents, experiencing trouble with their adopted children, came to me for counselling.

Typical of these were a husband and wife, both committed Christians, both gentle and loving people, who had adopted a six-month-old baby girl ten years before. From the beginning, the infant was remarkably undemonstrative, refusing to be held and cuddled. Even when very small, she seemed filled with hostility and anger, rejecting all signs of affection by her adoptive parents. At the age of seven, she began to exhibit real cruelty, trying with deliberate calculation to hurt her parents. She was going on eleven when they sought me out.

As they talked, it suddenly became clear to me what the trouble probably was and that most of it must have occurred when the child was *in utero*. The couple sitting with me that day knew little of their child's natural mother, but what they knew (and what obtains in so many such cases) shed a great deal of light. The natural mother had become pregnant when she was a freshman in college. She was forced to leave college for a year, and that particular college, the one of her choice, refused to reinstate her. One can well imagine the anger and resentment the girl felt, which destructive emotions were visited upon the fetus.

After several sessions with the adoptive parents, I explained to them what the prayer for the healing of the memories was, and asked them to explain to the child as much as she was capable of comprehending. I then asked them to bring the little girl to me if they could do so without forcing her against her will.

Two weeks later they brought her. She was an attractive, albeit sullen, child. It became quickly evident that her emotional problems included deep feelings of rejection due to the fact that her natural mother had "given her away," as she put it. I explained to her that in the very beginning her mother was undoubtedly resentful and frightened, not knowing which way to turn. But I pointed out that she "loved you very much. She chose to have you, to give you life. When you were born she *had* to give you up because she loved you so much she wanted people to have you who could take very good care of you as she could not."

As the little girl had been given a good religious background, I spoke to her for a few minutes about Jesus, and then asked if I might pray for her. Noncommittedly she replied, "O.K. Go ahead."

I prayed that Jesus would go back in time to when this child was an embryo, asking that He touch that unborn baby and grant her the assurance that He loved her with an everlasting love. I prayed that He would give this baby the assurance that He had planned and wanted her to be born, and had known her name since the beginning of time. I prayed that He would grant her the certainty of mind that He had already chosen her adoptive parents, who would love her in His love. Then I asked Jesus to go to this child when she was an infant, taking her in His arms, saying, "I love you as much as though you were the only child in the entire world. Next to Me, your father and mother love you. So *accept* this love, my child. It will be yours forever, no matter what you do."

At each stage of this little girl's life, including the present, I prayed that He would assure her of His unbounded love as well as the love of her parents in whose care He has placed her. I prayed that Jesus would heal now all the hurts of this child and enable her to accept His love and that of her parents.

When the prayer was concluded, tears were streaming down the girl's face, and she said, "Please, would you pray just one more thing?" When I said, "Of course, what?" she replied, "Please ask Jesus to forgive me for being so mean to Mommie and Daddy."

The love of God filled that room, and I knew that in her as in so many others a marvelous healing had taken place. From that day on, she manifested to her parents a new gentleness and an increasing receptivity to their love.

This sort of healing is not restricted to adopted children. Many adults have suffered the emotional consequences of being unwanted by their married parents. In most cases, after they were born, they were much loved and had happy childhoods. However, damage had been done while they were in the fetal stage, which had to be healed before they, as adults, could be whole.

Two questions recur pertaining to prayer for the healing of memories. The first: "Can I pray this prayer for *myself?*" The answer is "Yes," but in my experience this must be qualified by the comment that it seems more effective when prayed by someone else.

The second question is "Can I, as an intercessor, pray this prayer for someone else?"

For a long while I honestly did not know the answer. Only recently have I noted that in three successive cases this has been successfully done. In two of these three cases, the prayer was offered without the knowledge of the one prayed for. Generally speaking, however, it appears to be more effective to pray directly with the person concerned, and regardless of the reason for intercession, it is helpful if the person knows he or she is being prayed for and when.

Later

When I went over to the convent at noon to pick up my mail, I was stopped by a woman visiting us for a few days. She asked for prayer, telling me that she suffered from severe arthritis and was in pain.

My mind still on the healing of the unconscious mind, I spoke to her of a way of prayer I have found effective in many cases of painful, chronic ailments like arthritis. Someone who suffers from such an ailment, for example, knows that if he moves in a certain way, extreme pain will result. No matter how certain of Christ's healing power the sufferer may be, his knowledge of increased pain under certain conditions tends to dominate his mind, both conscious and unconscious. In the present case, I prayed that her *fear* of pain, which was based on experiential knowledge and thus in her unconscious mind was truth, might be totally eradicated and overcome by that greater Truth who is Jesus. This prayer we can effectively pray for ourselves as often as necessary.

As a follow-up exercise, I suggested to her, as I do to all who suffer, that she pray for the relief of pain for five minutes at a time in the beginning. So short a period of surcease is often acceptable to the mind which cannot, at first, accept total healing. This time can gradually be increased until, as frequently happens, the patient is entirely healed. In order to avoid concentration on self, it is important that the individual concerned use the pain-free period to offer praise to God and to pray for others.

During his earthly ministry, Jesus healed in many different ways, perceiving that which was the primary need. For example, a paralyzed man is brought to our Lord because he wants to walk. The first words Jesus says to him are: "Son, your sins are forgiven." Then and only then, does He say to the helpless man, "Stand up! Roll up your mat and go home" (Mt. 9:2).

And so it is today. Jesus knows what kind of healing is required, regardless of what we think may be our need.

A Roman Catholic nun attending a healing service told me her story on her way out of the church.

Now over fifty years old, she had come to the service stone deaf in her left ear, praying that the ear would be opened that she might hear again. She had been deafened at the age of four when her father, in an uncontrollable rage, struck a blow to her head which ruptured her eardrum. She had never been able to forgive him. While at the altar rail, she experienced a great surge of love for her father. At long last she was able to forgive.

She arose from her knees completely forgetting the physical healing she had desired, thanking God for His mercy in liberating her from her resentment of her father's act. As she put it, "I felt 'clean' all over."

She resumed her seat on the aisle, sitting next to the two sisters with whom she had come. The one on her left whispered to her and she nodded. It was then that she realized that her ear had been opened and her hearing totally restored.

I ponder Saint Paul's admonition in his letter to Timothy: "O Timothy, guard what has been committed to you" (1 Tim. 6:20). I take it to myself, and fall asleep.

6.

Appointment with God: Prayer as Companionship

I awoke shivering. Turning up the electric blanket, I snuggled deeply into its warmth and switched on the weather radio just in time in hear: "The temperature at 4:00 A.M. was minus twenty-five degrees." At this news I was strongly tempted to remain in my warm bed, say my prayers, and skip going out into the pitch black, frigid cold to mass.

I thought of the verse in one of the psalms we say daily at Lauds: "Let the saints be joyful with glory: let them rejoice in their beds" (149:5). *This* morning I felt like rejoicing in *my bed!* But again, as always when similarly tempted, there flashed through my mind the parable of the Banquet, and the feeble excuses of those invited as to why they could not attend (Lk. 14:16-20). And besides, this is an important holy day. Mary and Joseph, obedient in all things, present Jesus in the Temple following the Law of Moses: "Every first-born male shall be consecrated to the Lord" (Lk. 2:23). So of course I went, bundled up with two sweaters under my fur coat and a wool scarf over my face, leaving only my eyes uncovered. "O ye frost and cold, bless ye the Lord; O ye ice and snow, bless ye the Lord; praise him and magnify him forever" (Song of the Three Young Men).

Despite the cold, my heart sang on the way home, echoing the words of Simeon: "Lord, now lettest thou thy servant depart in peace, according to thy word; for mine eyes have seen thy salvation which thou hast prepared in the presence of all peoples, a light for revelation to the Gentiles, and for glory to thy people Israel" (Lk. 2:29–32 RSV).

Yesterday someone came to me for help in her prayer life. This is probably why, today, I find myself reflecting on prayer: what I have learned through experience and what I have yet to learn.

Just now the words seem to ring in my ears: "Choose life, then, . . . by loving the Lord, your God, heeding his voice, and holding fast to him. For that will mean life for you" (Dt. 30:19–20). To "heed" His voice, we have first to hear it; and to hear it, we pray and *listen.* In fact, I reflect, listening may well be the most important part of prayer.

Our vocal prayers of adoration, thanksgiving, penitence, intercession, and petition, our "flash" prayers throughout the day, are all necessary and good. The offices, the liturgy, are far more than words read out of a book. They are the prayers of the Church continuously being offered throughout the world. The Church at prayer—the whole world and its future depends on this. However, in all such prayer, it is we who do the talking. Listening prayer is something else again—and vital to our spiritual welfare, that we may be obedient to God and thus, as His people and members of the Body, may strengthen the Church. It is only by listening that we are able to hear His voice which, at least for a short time each day, is not drowned out by the strident cacophony of the world. In the noisy activism of our environment, that still, small voice needs the quietude of heart and mind if it is to be audible.

My counselee remarked upon the difficulty of being quiet and just listening. She is right. Interior silence is difficult to achieve, and exterior silence frightens us. For the most part, we do not know how to handle it, let alone use it. Yet, until we learn, deep prayer is impossible.

I think today with special gratitude of the great spiritual masters who have taught me so much of prayer and of the spiritual life: Saint Teresa of Avila, Saint John of the Cross, Saint Ignatius

Loyola, Saint Francis of Assisi, Saint Augustine, Saint Thomas Aquinas, Saint Francis de Sales, the eighteenth-century Jesuit Jean Pierre de Caussade (the greatest spiritual director I have ever had), and all the rest. The core of their teaching is as relevant today as when they lived on earth. This morning they pass before my eyes, a company of holy men and women to whom I owe so much, and without whom my life would have been immeasurably impoverished.

Nevertheless and paradoxically, the complicated structure of meditation so many of them taught in the Middle Ages, proved to me a stumbling block for a long time. It was years before I learned that on the printed page their individual methods appeared far more complicated than they actually were. Just as it was years before I really comprehended Saint Teresa's metaphor of water in describing her own stages of prayer, and Saint John's "Dark Night of the Soul," while the Ignatian Exercises seemed to me impossibly rigid until I came to understand that his way of prayer was never meant to be totally inflexible.

For years the words "meditation" and "mental prayer" conjured up in my mind a system of intellectual gymnastics instead of that deep, quiet reflection which leads to the "conversation with Christ" of which Saint Teresa speaks. I finally learned to sift the wheat from the chaff (the latter of my own making), and I also came to learn the value of *some* structure as we begin to pray, a structure which need not be complicated and must be adapted to the individual pray-er. As I reminded my counselee, none of us prays in precisely the same way, for "God leads every soul by a separate path."[1] We all have attractions to particular kinds of prayer. Sometimes these can be a trap, but they keep us from a way of prayer which may seem difficult to us at first.

Yesterday my friend asked, "Where should I meditate? In a church?" If one is able, a church is a good place, as interruptions are fewer than at home, and a church tends to be hallowed by the prayers of the faithful. However, it most certainly is not necessary to pray always in a church. I remember how, long ago, imbued with the Desert Fathers, I created my own "desert" to which I could retreat. And I learned then the value of praying in the same place every day.

In the beginning, my "desert" was my favorite chair in a corner of the living room. I found it helpful to set up a small table facing me, on which I placed a cross or a crucifix or a picture of Jesus. To close my eyes seemed to invite an onrush of distractions with which I could not cope. Focusing my eyes on a religious object helped me to concentrate. The distractions ("What shall I have for dinner tonight?" "Oh dear, it's raining. I wonder if the children remembered their umbrellas") only *poured* in now; they did not *rush!* I learned not to fight them, for that gave them a force they should not have. I just tried to ignore them, and gently draw myself back to prayer. My prayer often seemed to consist largely of bringing myself back to prayer. (In all honesty, there are still times when this is true.)

When I finished my own meditation today, I recalled how my counselee had asked, "What should I meditate *on?*" Scripture is the primary source, though the Lord's Prayer, or the Creed, or spiritual reading provide endless sources for reflection.

I observed that a prerequisite of prayer is to immerse ourselves in Scripture. My friend nodded and told me that she was reading the Bible straight through from Genesis through the Book of Revelation. This has never worked for me. Most of us seem to do better if we follow some daily reading plan. The Episcopal Prayer Book contains a daily lectionary, while the Roman Catholic missalettes contain daily readings. Further, there are a number of excellent Bible reading plans.[2]

To follow such readings is to have daily material for meditation or, to use a less frightening word, reflection. Most spiritual directors suggest making one's meditation in the morning when one is fresh. My own experience has taught me that the time of meditation must depend upon the life style of the individual. I do, however, suggest, that the material for meditation be read the preceding night. Personally I have found it helpful to do this in bed shortly before going to sleep. The Scripture thus read seems to work on the unconscious mind during sleep, providing the yeast for prayer the following day. (In traditional language, this is known as remote preparation.)

The next day when it is time to go to prayer, I advise disconnecting your telephone if you possibly can. Then retreat to your "desert." Before you actually begin to pray, prepare yourself as you will. I invariably ask for the guidance of the Holy Spirit and His illumination of the material chosen. Since in prayer we offer our entire beings to God, I adapt the prayer of Ignatius for my own: "Take and receive, O Lord, my entire liberty, my memory, my understanding, my whole will. All that I am, all that I have, You have given me. I give it back again to you now, to be used according to Your own good purpose." (This is known as the immediate preparation.) Then read slowly and thoughtfully the material selected and begin your meditation.

I cautioned my counselee, who is a scholar, that the *devotional* use of the Bible is very different from *study*. To try to exegete the passage is death to the spirit of prayer! You are in no hurry, and if the first sentence should "jump out" at you, stay with it for the entire time of the meditation if you so desire.

If you have chosen a Gospel passage, reflect upon what Jesus is saying to you. If you wish, make yourself part of, and a participant in, the scene depicted. However, you do not *have* to do this. The important thing to remember is the fundamental rule of prayer enunciated by Teresa, when she states that prayer consists not in *thinking* much but in *loving* much. To still one's mind, to talk little and to listen hard—this constitutes a way of prayer which can lead to union with God.

Talk with our Lord about the material you have just read. Employ in your conversation with Him, adoration, thanksgiving, sorrow for sin. As we can offer any act of prayer such as the Our Father as an act of intercession for many, so can we use part of this prayer time for intercession, bringing before Him those who have a special need. We need not voice this need, only relinquish those for whom we pray and their situations to God, offering ourselves to be used as channels for His grace.

I recall cautioning my friend: This is a two-way conversation with God. Thus our prayer should be, "Speak, Lord"; and then, in silence, we listen. This colloquy with Jesus should be primarily an intimate union of friendship with Him, at the same time never forgetting that He is God.

The conclusion of our prayer time consists of thanking God for the graces we have received, briefly examining our failings, and promising to try to eradicate them in the future. I like to end it all with the Our Father. I have found this general conclusion of prayer more satisfactory than the traditional "gathering up the fruits of our prayer" and making a definite resolution which we offer to God. For me, there often are no immediately discernible fruits. These are more apt to be cumulative. However, as I explained to my counselee, all of this is flexible, as is my personal custom of leaving five or ten minutes of the meditation time to *write* the conclusion of the prayer. These I call my "Letters to the Lord," and keep them in a notebook as part of a spiritual journal.

No one method can solve all the problems of mental prayer nor, I think, are they meant to be solved. There will always be distractions and undoubtedly periods of dryness or aridity, times when God seems very far away, and our prayers seem to hit the ceiling and bounce back. According to Dom Chapman, it is when these things do *not* occur that we have cause to worry. As he says, "Embrace aridities and distractions and temptations, and you will find you love to be in darkness." He then goes on to say, "Remember that a distracted prayer is generally more humbling than a recollected prayer—therefore it gives more glory to God and less to us."[3]

My mind reverts now to the many who have asked, "But how do you pray when you *can't?*" For those times when prayer seems impossible because of dryness or illness or great spiritual fatigue, I find it helpful to make some of the great prayers of the Church my own. There are various good collections of these.[4] Also—and especially for those unused to quiet, reflective prayer—the "plan" of Cardinal Mercier has proved helpful. "For five minutes each day," he suggests, "quiet your imagination, shut your eyes to all things of the senses, and close your ears to all sounds of earth, so as to be able to withdraw into the sanctuary of your baptized soul which is the temple of the Holy Spirit. Then say: 'O Holy Spirit, soul of my soul, I adore Thee. Enlighten, strengthen, and console me. Tell me what I ought to do and command me to do it. I promise to be submissive in everything Thou permittest to happen to me. Only show me what is Thy will.' Your life will pass happily and serenely and consolation will abound even in the midst of troubles. Grace will be given in proportion to the trials, as well as the strength to bear them."

Yesterday after we had talked of prayer, my counselee asked the common question, "How long should I meditate?" I suggested fifteen minutes working up to thirty minutes or more as she felt led. However long a period is set aside, it should be kept inviolate insofar as is humanly possible. Although we set a definite time for meditation, the essence of prayer—namely, a state of recollection and humility, our hearts speaking to the Heart of Christ—should be carried over into and through our entire lives. Saint Teresa calls mental prayer the "royal highway to heaven." If we ourselves embark on this highway, we take others with us. As we can only keep Christ by giving Him, so the more of Him we have the more we have to give.

"What about physical posture in prayer?" she asked. I always advise a comfortable position, but not so comfortable that we go to sleep, and certainly not so uncomfortable that our minds are focused on hurting knees and aching backs rather than on Him to whom we pray! I have long done much of my praying flat on my back, and was glad to note that Ignatius recommends this.

If one should be immersed in Scripture in order to pray well, so also should one be saturated in Christ. One way to achieve the latter is to learn the use of the ancient Jesus Prayer, "Lord Jesus Christ, Son of God, have mercy on me a sinner." If this prayer is repeated often enough, day after day and month after month, it becomes the silent and ceaseless prayer of the heart it is intended to be. Another use of the name of Jesus, probably derived from the Jesus Prayer, is the Rosary of the Holy Name. In this devotion, we repeat the name of Jesus, very slowly, ten times, concluding each decade with a short prayer, such as, "I worship You"; "Have mercy"; "Open my ears that I may hear Your voice." There is power in His name as attested by the early Church Fathers, and as I have discovered in my work in the healing ministry. The repetition of the name is neither "vain" nor mindless. Implicit in the name of Jesus is Jesus Himself, His personality, His attributes, the power of the living Christ. It is in the intervals of silence between the repetitions of the Holy Name, that I most clearly hear His voice.

"Prayer oneth the soul to God," says Julian of Norwich. Yes, and this is the goal of all prayer.

"Prayer is presence and companionship, however dark and troubled, or however lithe and lovely this companionship may be."[5] For me, "Prayer is presence" defines prayer. Sometimes in the dark, the companionship may be difficult and discouraging. It is in these times that I think of the cloud: a cloud of forgetting behind, a cloud of unknowing ahead. And for the present, hanging on by one's fingernails through sheer faith.

When all is said and done, prayer is simply being with God. It is being with Someone you love very much, in a profound, abiding companionship where verbal communication and active thought are unnecessary. As there is a sense of wonder between two people who are deeply in love, so now is that wonder increased a thousandfold and augmented by total awe as we fully realize in whose presence we are.

Our minds centered on Him, our hearts both sanctuary and altar, we gaze wordlessly on the Beloved. This is prayer.

"God, in Thy godeness give me Thyself, for only in Thee have I all" (Julian of Norwich).

Late Afternoon

Early tomorrow my plane takes off for a warmer climate. The roads here are slick with ice; it is snowing hard, and the airport threatens to close down. One does not just "miss" missions scheduled far in advance, so to be as safe as possible I have just reserved a room for tonight at the airport motel. The driving conditions are already so bad that no taxis will risk the drive to the airport. Two intrepid and very kind sisters have offered to take me. We leave in just a few minutes. After all this, I hope planes will be taking off in the morning.

"All shall be well and all shall be well, and all manner of things shall be well" (Julian of Norwich). Amen! And now to close my bags and put on my coat.

7.

Celebrating Lent

Today is the first day of Lent and we received the imposition of ashes. Since the ninth century this rite has symbolized the penitence of the people of God. I keep hearing the words of the prayer: "Almighty God, . . . Grant that these ashes may be to us a sign of our mortality and penitence, that we may remember that it is only by your gracious gift that we are given everlasting life; through Jesus Christ our Savior."*

The first time I heard the term "celebrating" Lent, it seemed to me incongruous to "celebrate" that season set apart by the Church for penance. However, as I reflected upon it, it came to make good sense. Lent is an old English word meaning "spring," and spring is a time of growth and increase. This is certainly cause for celebration, as is the fact that although Lent and Holy Week take us through the crucifixion, each passing day also brings us closer to the incredibly wonderful event upon which the faith is founded: the Resurrection.

Resurrection. This word can apply to each day of our lives as we are risen again in the faith. It is the light which continually beckons us onward, the light which gives us courage to go on, no matter how great our suffering or affliction, for we know that after Good Friday comes Easter. And we also know that without a Good Friday there can *be* no Easter.

My mind flies back to that trip to the airport which, thanks be to God, was open. So, mission accomplished! When the sisters and I

* The Book of Common Prayer (1979 edition), p. 265; hereafter cited as BCP.

finally got to the motel I could not even treat them to a cup of coffee to fortify them for the long and hazardous trip back to the convent. Apparently everyone in Cincinnati had my idea of spending the night near the airport. Not only was there no place to park, but cars were backed up for a good mile, inching their way to the front entrance of the motel. I must have got one of the last available rooms, for the lobby was bedlam. People were being turned away by the score, pleading for the privilege of spending the night in the lobby.

It was a good mission with many healings, but curiously, what remains most vividly in my mind are the morning discussion periods. These were dominated by a theme initiated by a young married woman in a wheelchair, incapacitated by multiple sclerosis. It was she who asked the first question: "If I am not healed, how can I possibly glorify God? I can't take care of my family. I can't do *anything* but sit in a wheelchair." This same question was immediately echoed by others who for one reason or another, whether because of age, illness, or young children whom they could not leave, felt they were not able to serve God as actively as they felt they should.

If I were granted one wish in regard to my work in the healing ministry, it would be that I might convey the certainty I feel that no matter what our condition, we are all within God's providence and that He is always in charge. If I could just convey my conviction that the important thing is to "be" and not to "do." The only time God cannot use us is if we make ourselves unavailable. Physical handicaps, illness, family circumstances give none of us the right to say "no" to God. Regardless of our personal situation we can offer ourselves, knowing that He will consecrate what we dedicate to Him. In this era of frenetic activism, it is God alone who enables us, so long as we draw a breath, to live in the constant process of becoming.

I know, beyond the shadow of a doubt, that whether we are flat on our backs awaiting healing or in perfect health, He will enable us to serve Him as He wills, perhaps to pray for those in need, perhaps to lend a sympathetic ear to those who need to talk, perhaps to attend healing services regularly to pray for, and bolster the faith of, others. I have learned both in my own life and by observation that the promise God made to Paul He has made to us, a promise He never fails to fulfill, namely, that His grace is *always* sufficient, that His strength *is* made perfect in weakness, for it is then that the power of Christ rests upon us (2 Cor. 12:9).

We believe that God will make us whole, but while we wait, there is important work for us to do. I asked the young woman in the wheelchair to invite God to work in her, assuring her that if she did, there would be a great change in her life, that others would notice this change, and she would be an inspiration to all who came in contact with her.

I remember a man recovering from deep depression who asked, "How could *I* possibly help anyone?" Anyone who has suffered from clinical depression can be of inestimable assistance to others who are enduring the same suffering, a suffering which no one who has not undergone it can fully understand. *I* cannot understand it, but having seen so much of the agony it causes, I feel great compassion for its victims. However, I daresay those who have actually been through it could be more helpful to others in the same situation than can I. "He cannot heal who has not suffered much; for only sorrow, sorrow understands."[1]

"Do not live in fear, little flock. It has pleased your Father to give you the kingdom" (Lk. 12:32). By being totally open to His reign we can all, regardless of our state, achieve undreamed-of heights in the life of the spirit, as His kingdom gradually is realized in each one of us.

I glimpsed this kingdom in the making, as I looked out over the people in the chapel. I saw that peace which passes understanding on the face of the man who was emerging from his depression. I saw in the face of the woman with young children a radiance lit by her resolution to serve God joyfully within her present circumstances. I saw in the eyes of the woman with multiple sclerosis no longer fear but now a quiet trust, derived from her knowledge that God is indeed in charge of her life.

I was overjoyed (those who had planned a lovely luncheon for me that day, alas were not, for I missed it!) when at the end of the final discussion time several people asked if they could go to the altar rail to dedicate themselves anew to God. It ended with the entire chapel going forward, and I knew the rejoicing there must have been in heaven as these people of God offered their lives to Him, made holy through their self-relinquishment.

Thinking back to this, I reflect on what I learned long ago, that the best assurance of healing lies in willingness to remain *unhealed* if only we may have more of God. More recently I learned the blessing of holy indifference. I believe the persons at the altar rail that morning intuitively comprehended this.

I see a subtle difference between what I choose to term holy indifference and resignation or relinquishment of oneself to God's will. The latter seems to imply a certain reluctance or personal struggle as we attempt to align our wills with His, whereas holy indifference is to actually *will* the will of God. This came clear to me during a period when I was praying hard and long over several situations. One day I found myself saying, "Lord, I honestly don't care any more what the outcome is. The only thing I really want is that your will be done. So do with me, in this situation, as You will, and I am content." To my own surprise, I found that I was! This kind of prayer springs from an attitude of holy indifference, an attitude which can only be achieved by our own desire and God's grace. Then, and only then, can we say, "I asked God for strength that I might achieve; I was made weak that I might learn humbly to obey. I asked for health that I might do greater things; I was given infirmity that I might do better things. I asked for riches that I might be happy; I was given poverty that I might be wise. I asked for power that I might have the praise of men; I was given weakness that I might feel the need of God. I asked for all things that I might enjoy life; I was given life that I might enjoy all things. I got nothing that I asked for, but everything I had hoped for. Almost despite myself, my unspoken prayers were answered. . . . I am, among all men, most richly blessed!" (Anonymous).

Later

I just picked up my mail, and of all coincidences, there is a letter from the young woman with multiple sclerosis. She writes, "I feel like a different person and am sure God is at work within me." The joy reflected in her letter makes clear that in His name and by the power of the Spirit, her victory is won. She has heard and understood, and I praise God!

I think again of the exhortation given this morning by the chaplain before the imposition of ashes: "I invite you, therefore, in the name of the Church, to the observance of a holy Lent, by self-examination and repentance; by prayer, fasting and self-denial; and by reading and meditating on God's holy Word." (BCP, p. 265). This seems to sum up very well what should constitute the Lenten discipline for the Christian.

Somewhere I read that more healings occur in Lent than at any other time of the year. This is not surprising, for the spiritual exercises suggested for Lent are precisely those which we emphasize for the establishment of a climate for healing. Further, they constitute in themselves the basis of a rule by which the Christian lives if he would advance in the life of the spirit.

If we are not already living by rule, Lent is a good time to start, using the Lenten discipline as a firm foundation. Most Christians are familiar with everything contained in the Lenten "invitation" with the possible exception of fasting. Fasting is of such importance that I continually wonder why so little attention is paid to it. Jesus gave us specific instructions: "How can wedding guests go in mourning so long as the groom is with them? When the day comes that the groom is taken away, then they will fast" (Mt. 9:15).

In the coming of Jesus, the reign of God came among His disciples as a present power. The Bridegroom was in their midst, so obviously it was a time for *feasting*, not *fasting*. There would come a time, however, for His disciples to fast. That time is now for those of us who attempt to follow Him.

During the last mission, someone said to me, "My father is dying. I'm fasting so that God will heal him." But we do not fast as a means of bargaining with God, as a means of getting Him to do what we want! Like Anna, the prophetess, we *worship* God in fasting and prayer. Fasting as a spiritual exercise must be done with our eyes on Him; for only one reason, love of God; and for only one purpose, to glorify Him.

The biblical concept of fasting is to abstain from food. If one's physical condition does not permit this, there are other ways to abstain. I reflect that what at least used to be the customary Lenten fast, if observed now, is one of the reasons for the reputed increase of healings during this season. I suggest always that those who attend healing services come fasting as they are able. For working people, going all day without food may not be practicable. In such cases I suggest a very light luncheon, and nothing more to eat until after the service. The ideal fast is, in my opinion, of twenty-four hours duration. Water, coffee, or tea are permissible.

Using the Ash Wednesday exhortation as the basis for a rule, I would add spiritual reading in addition to the Bible. This should not be controversial, as when controversy comes in the door, the spirit of prayer flies out the window. For this reason, I prefer to confine my own spiritual reading, as such, to the classics. Whatever material has been selected should be read slowly and reflectively.

Baron von Hugel, well-known spiritual director (Evelyn Underhill was under his direction), advised fifteen minutes daily of devotional reading. He kept at his bedside three books: the Bible, *The Imitation of Christ*, and *The Confessions of St. Augustine.* (I keep on my bedtable the Bible, *The Imitation* and *The Cloud of Unknowing.*) Although a voracious reader, his strictly devotional reading usually was limited to only fifteen minutes. "That daily quarter of an hour for now forty years or more," he writes, "has been one of the great sustenances and sources of calm for my life."[2] While he does not limit those under his direction to fifteen minutes, he urges that they read not more than fifteen minutes at one time, for otherwise, he observes, "You would sink to ordinary reading."

I suggested to "my" people at Saint Thomas on Monday night that during Lent they might wish to increase every aspect of their rule by five minutes each day: five minutes more of prayer, of Scripture reading, of spiritual reading. I told them, too, of an exercise in which I sometimes engage during Lent, namely, I go through the Psalms (amazing how many prefigure Christ!) copying from each one those verses which are particularly meaningful to me. Then I string my favorite verses all together. In doing this, I find how much I memorize so that throughout the year, I have at my fingertips those verses that I want at any given time. I also mark passages from the Gospels, memorizing them.

Every Lent I vow that some day when I have nothing but time on my hands, I will put together my favorite translations of every verse of both Old and New Testaments. Of course, I never shall, for it would take a lifetime, but I certainly would enjoy having such a "Bible" for my own use! I suspect that many people have my trouble. They like some verses in one translation and some in another. The net result is having to work with five or six versions of the Bible, all accurate, but some more felicitously translated than others.

My Lents are often too filled with speaking. I remember some years ago when I asked my spiritual director if I could, in good conscience, refuse speaking engagements so that I could spend a good and quiet Lent. His answer was a firm "No," followed by, "Would you refuse to see someone in need because you happened to be praying when he came to your door?" My answer was, obviously, "Of course not." "Then," said my director, "you can't refuse to spread the Good News simply because *you* want to keep what you think is a 'good' Lent."

I have remembered this over the years, and I know he was right. In thinking of it now, I am reminded of the legend of the hermit who had a vision one night, in which he was told that Jesus would come to visit him on a certain day. When that day came, the hermit awoke in joyful expectation. He began to pray early in the morning and prayed all day. He was interrupted at seven o'clock that evening, when a small child came to his door, crying with hunger and asking for a crust of bread. The hermit replied testily, "Go away! Can't you see I'm praying?" whereupon he shut the door in the child's face. He continued his prayers hour after hour, and when midnight came and went, with no sign of our Lord's visit, the hermit cried aloud, "Lord, why have you not kept your promise? I have prayed all day and you have not come." Came the divine response, "My son, I came tonight at seven, but you slammed the door in my face."

This Lent I am going to make every effort to attend all the offices in the oratory at the convent. For far too long I have been so busy that I have had to spend most evenings on correspondence or cleaning or laundry. I have had to miss nearly all the noon and night offices. Although I read them at home, it is much better to go to the oratory.

I smile when people say to me, "It must be wonderful living at the convent and having nothing to do all day but *pray.*" (The sisters, too, would smile, as this is an active community, which runs Bethany School, Saint Mary's Memorial Home for the Retired, and offers many ecumenical retreats and quiet days.) Speaking for myself, I might wish that I had more time for prayer, other than having to make it by setting my alarm clock for four-thirty each morning.

Clergymen have told me that in most of their sermons they are preaching to themselves. I know what they mean. The night before last at Saint Thomas I suggested to "my" people various Lenten disciplines, and as I look now at my speaking calendar, I was distinctly preaching to *myself!*

8.

"According to Your Word"

I have a special feeling for Saint Gregory. In my last book I address myself to a particular form of intercession.[1] I urge those
who are suffering in any way, including pain from such things as
anxiety or frustration, to offer their brokenness to God, to be used
for His glory and on behalf of someone they know who is in need
of prayer. I suggest that they pray in their own words to this effect, "Lord, I offer to you my brokenness, praying that you will
convert this to your holy purpose and use it for your glory. I pray
also that you will use it on behalf of Mary or John whose need is so
great." I have found this to be an extremely powerful method of
intercession, which at the same time transforms the suffering of
the intercessor into a creative and redemptive thing.

I had long thought this way of prayer was my own discovery,
based on Col. 1:24. Then I learned that Saint Gregory had used
such a means of intercession nearly fourteen hundred years before
my time! This seems to be the case every time I think I have made
a new discovery in the spiritual life. Invariably I find that someone
else "discovered" it more than a thousand years ago. Recently I
was cheered to read a comment by a well-known theologian: "If
you think you have come up with a totally new idea, watch out:
you are probably in heresy!"

In regard to "new ideas," I seem also to share a difficulty expressed by Thomas Merton: "You find out that your latest discovery is something you already found out five years ago." Nevertheless it is profoundly true, as Merton says, "that one penetrates

deeper and deeper into the same ideas and the same experiences."[2]
In any event, much as I would love to study Scripture under St.
Jerome, so I would love to learn more of prayer from Gregory the
Great!

In view of the type of prayer I have been thinking about, and
considering the kind of winter we are having here, it is not surprising that my mind flies back to the last winter I was at Calvary
Church in Pittsburgh. One February night I was told that two bus
loads of people were coming from out of town to the healing service, and I had agreed to speak with them after the service. It was
an exceptionally long service, and by the time I was finished and
was ready to start home, it was after eleven-thirty.

On that bitterly cold night, the roads were thickly glazed with
ice. I was extremely tired, and having been on my feet for hours,
my back was hurting badly. About halfway home, and after three
unsuccessful tries at getting my car up what appeared to be a snow
bank (when cleared I knew it was a road), I began to offer my fatigue and aching back to God. I prayed that He would use them on
behalf of one of "my" people who was crippled by a bad back after
two unsuccessful operations. The poor man had not been at the
service that night, and I knew there must be a good reason for his
absence. By the time I reached home well after midnight, all
fatigue was forgotten as was my own aching back.

The person for whom I had offered my problems in union with
Christ was at Calvary the following Monday night. After the service he said, "The strangest thing happened last Monday night. I
couldn't come to the service, I was simply in too much pain. About
midnight, I suddenly had the sensation of being in a tub of hot
water. The pain in my back just seeped out. I could feel it leaving.
I went to sleep and woke up the next day without a vestige of pain,
and I've had none since." Coincidence? No. Not when this sort of
thing happens again and again.

Such intercession is one part of the prayer of reparation, in
which we pray especially for all those who withhold their love
from God, for all who do not pray, for all who have rejected Him.
We offer ourselves in union with Christ's sacrifice on the cross,
and thus share a tiny bit in the whole redemptive process. The
danger inherent in any prayer of reparation is a self-righteous atti-

tude. To avoid this, we have only to remember that if our Lord is wounded by the neglect of the unbeliever whom He longs to bring to Himself, the Sacred Heart is broken by the transgressions of those of us who profess to believe, yet withhold from Him the prayers and the love for which He thirsts.

It was in the seventeenth century that as Saint Margaret Mary was praying this prayer our Lord came to her in a vision. He asked her to spend the hour between eleven o'clock and midnight every Thursday, prostrate, in union with His agony at Gethsemane, for all who rejected Him. This vision led to the establishment of the Holy Hour which many of us observe today. It is an hour of adoration and intercession which can be observed at home or in church, and on any day and at any hour which is convenient.

Today is my wedding anniversary as well as a feast day. I dreamt last night of my late husband. What a lovely anniversary present! In my dream, Alvin was running toward me, arms outstretched, with a look of ineffable joy on his face. I ran to meet him, but just before I reached him, he suddenly paused and held up his hands to stop me. I saw him turn his head as if listening to someone behind him. And then I heard him say, as if in answer, "Not yet?" Slowly he turned back toward me, smiled, and shook his head. There was an indefinable promise in that smile, and as I awoke, I knew that Alvin would be there to meet me when the time came.

I suppose at this time of year, when we meditate particularly intensely on our Lord's passion during Lent, that it is not unusual to think of death.

Clearing off my desk this morning, I reread a letter from Father Paul, a Franciscan friar who has long been a beloved friend and my spiritual director. As if reading it for the first time, I was blinded by tears.

Written at two o'clock in the morning, he says in part: "I

returned today (more accurately *yesterday*) from the hospital where I had an emergency prostate operation. Cancer, of course. They did a 'scan' and apparently every bone in my body has been invaded by cancer, and there is a large tumor on my left kidney.

"Needless to say this is a great joy to me. Now I can see the end of the road. The long night is over and the dawn is near. It may be some time coming, but I can wait because it has an end in His love, and I know He loves me.

"As I've said so often, for me, to die is to be going home for Christmas. And whatever time it comes, it will be Christmas for me, with bells ringing, incense so thick you can't see the altar, and everyone's heart light, glowing and happy, because the Child is here.

"My surgeon says he will ease the pain as much as possible and he will *not* extend my life artificially. I love him for that. Now, Emily, *you* please promise me that you won't pray for my healing on this earth. God bless."

Of course I have given him my word, but have also told him that I could not agree not to pray that he might be spared suffering.

The promise I gave is not hard to keep. His is the Christian response to death. For while I believe with all my heart that it is our holy obligation to do all that we can both medically (within reason) and spiritually (without limitation) to preserve God's first gift to us, our life, still it is only through death that any of us can be completely whole. For the Christian, death should never be regarded as the final disaster but rather the ultimate triumph. Father Paul has lived a long, full, and creative life. He has touched innumerable lives, and as an unsurpassed retreat conductor and spiritual director, he has led many, including me, along the way. I weep for myself that his life is drawing to a close, but my joy for him transcends my own grief. In sure and certain hope of the resurrection. . . .

Sister Virgina, always so strong and robust, is not looking well and seems strangely lacking in energy. We sit on opposite sides of the oratory, but I can always hear her clear voice above the others during Lauds. This morning even her voice sounded weak. I am concerned about her.

March 25
The Annunciation

Walking home from mass this morning, I marvelled at how, overnight, everything seems to have sprung to life. Snow two days ago—and suddenly it's spring. The convent grounds are bright with the shining gold of forsythia and daffodils, and the magnolias are about to burst into bloom. Everything this month seems to emphasize death and resurrection.

I love this feast day because I love Mary, Mother of our Lord; Mary, Star of the Sea. (For anyone who loves the sea as I do, I smile at God's determination to keep me from it. Brought up in New York in an era when anything west of Fifth Avenue was beyond the pale, I thought Pittsburgh, when we first moved there, was no man's land. Now it seems the "East," as I find myself in Cincinnati, indisputedly the Middle West.)

Mary is the perfect example of human obedience to God. I think of that young Jewish girl two thousands years ago, and how frightened she must have been at the awesome responsibility given her, to carry in her womb Jesus, the Son of God. I think of her unhesitating response to the angel Gabriel, "Behold, I am the handmaid of the Lord; let it be to me according to your word" (Lk. 1:38 RSV). Mary, the one whose supreme act of acquiescence to His will, changed the world for all people and for all time.

In the past, among certain factions of the Roman Catholic Church, there was a decided overemphasis on devotion to Mary: a time when she was mentioned by some as Co-Redemptrix. However, since the days of Vatican II which cautioned against such overemphasis, the official stance of this Church has been balanced. Yet the Protestant churches, in general, continue their rebellion against a past overemphasis by totally ignoring her. This is a curious phenomenon, because those churches which claim to be most solidly founded on the Bible seemingly choose to overlook Scripture altogether as it pertains to Mary. "Henceforth all generations will call me blessed" (Lk. 1:48 RSV). This is the written Word.

I remember with considerable amusement the first time I spoke on the subject of Mary. It was early in the ministry at Calvary in Pittsburgh. As the participating Episcopal priest and I were talking shortly before time for the healing service to begin, he said to me, "What are you preaching about tonight?" When I told him, he blanched. "Emily, you *can't,*" he said. "This is a *very* Protestant congregation. They won't accept it."

I replied, "I think they will. These people know their Bible. They've just overlooked the references to Mary, the way all of our churches have until recently 'overlooked' the significance and relevance of our Lord's earthly healing ministry."

I must admit that when I stepped into the pulpit that night, my heart somewhat quailed. Looking out over the congregation, the church seemed filled with Protestant clergy, some of whom I knew and loved, and others whom I knew at least by sight. Not to be daunted, I went ahead as planned. At the end of the service, these men came up to me as a group, unreservedly enthusiastic about the sermon they had just heard. All but one asked me for my notes, and for permission to preach the same sermon at their respective churches the next Sunday. I gladly gave it, had my notes typed up, and sent each one a mimeographed copy.

Where else but in the healing ministry could one preach one night on the Blessed Virgin and the next on "Pleading the Blood" and be equally well understood on both nights?

Devotion (not worship) to Mary as the Mother of our Redeemer is almost as old as the Church herself. Pictures drawn on the walls of the catacombs attest to this, while the belief in the efficacy of her intercessions is extremely ancient.

One difficulty for many Protestants, which I recognize and respect, is the fact that they do not believe that the saints, both living *and* dead, pray for us. This being so, they obviously cannot accept Mary as preeminent among the heavenly intercessors: preeminent because of her sanctity and thus the power of her prayers; the closest to her Son and therefore sharing a special place beside Him; the

Queen of Heaven, above angels and archangels and all the saints. However, rejection of Mary as intercessor does not preclude honoring her as the Mother of God.

"The Mother of God?" someone said to me. "That is *ridiculous!*" But it is not. "Who was she the mother *of?*" I countered. "Why, Jesus, of course," came the reply. Precisely. And Jesus was truly God as well as truly man. Notwithstanding, many non-Roman Catholics seem to feel more comfortable with the term *Theotokos,* God-bearer, used by the Eastern Church.

I readily admit that for a long time after I became a Christian, I had difficulty knowing what to "do" with Mary. I wanted no one, not even His Mother, to come between me and Jesus. I was to learn much from a seventeen-year-old girl, not a Roman Catholic, who was dying of leukemia. The closer to death she came, the closer her relationship with the Holy Mother. I pondered this for a long time and finally came to understand.

I did not have to contend with a personal disbelief in the prayers of the dead for us who live (or ours for them) as my Church teaches, and I unfeignedly believe, that the intercessions of our beloved dead (or as I think of them, our beloved "alive") have great efficacy. As I ask people here on earth to pray, so do I ask those nearest the Source of all power. Nevertheless, regardless of how any of us may believe in this particular area, the important thing for all of us to know, is that Christ forever lives to make intercession (Heb. 7:25), while the Holy Spirit intercedes for us as God wills (Rom. 8:27).

Whatever we may or may not believe about the Mother of our Lord, it is essential, as Christians, that we believe in the Virgin Birth.

"I can't see that it matters one way or the other," a young clergyman said to me not long ago. It matters very much indeed.

How would the Incarnation have come about, otherwise? How could Jesus have been fully God, if not conceived by the Holy Spirit? How fully man, if not born of woman? What would have happened to our salvation had Mary said to the messenger of the Lord, "No, thank you. I don't care to bear in my womb the Son of God conceived by the Holy Spirit?"

But the answer of this young girl to what must have been a terrifying proposal, was an unreserved "Yes."

God took the initiative with her, as He does with us. He is *able* to do it all, but unless we acquiesce as did Mary, the Almighty and All-powerful God has chosen to make Himself impotent in our lives.

"Let it be to me according to your word." This is a perfect healing prayer, denoting complete acquiescence to His will and the acknowledgment that, according to the written Word, it is for our wholeness, however this is to come about.

Pray this prayer often, and our souls will indeed magnify the Lord and our spirits rejoice in God, our Savior (Lk. 1:46, 47 RSV).

Pray this prayer and God will honor it, and we will know beyond the shadow of any doubt that His mercy is indeed on them that fear Him throughout all generations (Lk. 1:50).

It is late, and four-thirty comes awfully quickly!

Hail Mary, O favored one, the Lord is with you. Blessed are you among women and blessed is the fruit of your womb, Jesus (Lk. 1:28, 42 RSV). Pray for my children and all children everywhere this night.

Into your hands, O Lord, I commend my spirit, and all those who suffer. Bless and heal, dear Lord, and may your will be done on earth as it is in heaven.

9.

Life After Death

L ast night the temperature unexpectedly dropped to way below freezing and, alas, the lovely blossoms on the magnolia tree outside my window have been killed. The tree stands bereft and dejected, curiously symbolic of the hearts of Christendom as we begin the commemoration of the most solemn events of the Christian year. For today the Holy Triduum has begun, those last three days before Easter when we not only remember the passion but participate as best we can in the suffering and death of Christ.

It is evening and I have just returned from mass. I feel chilly though the house is warm, so I make a cup of hot coffee. I reflect upon the service tonight, which seems to me in a very real sense to be our Lord's last will and testament. All that He has taught for the three years of His earthly ministry, He has summarized at the Last Supper.

The institution of the Sacrament of His Body and Blood: "Mercifully grant that we may receive it thankfully in remembrance of Jesus Christ our Lord, who in these holy mysteries gives us a pledge of eternal life" (BCP, p. 274).

The washing of His disciples' feet: "Do you understand what I just did for you? . . . What I just did was to give you an example: as I have done, so you must do" (Jn. 13:12, 15). For, Jesus said, "This is my commandment: love one another as I have loved you" (Jn. 15:12).

And, finally: "Peace is my farewell to you, my peace is my gift to you" (Jn. 14:27). This is His gift of salvation.

After receiving Communion, a portion of the consecrated bread and wine is carried to the altar of repose, which is in the tiny side chapel of Saint Francis. The altar is stripped, the sanctuary light extinguished, and the church left in total darkness. The Light of the world has been put out, and people just like me have done it. Christ have mercy.

It is time now to return to the little chapel to keep my hour of the vigil. There is room for only three at a time, one on each side of the chapel, and one kneeling in the center before the altar. The two sisters and I who have this hour together, silently meet, and wait to replace those who are concluding their hour of prayer. At midnight the reserved Sacrament is placed in the tabernacle, and the chapel vigil is terminated.

It has started to rain hard, which somehow seems fitting. I wish I had kept a better Lent, done more praying instead of, as seems to be the case each year, doing more work.

Good Friday

The sound of trains in the night, usually pleasantly nostalgic, seemed unbearably sad last night.

Today we have the Mass of the Presanctified, celebrated since the seventh century. Immediately preceding this is the Veneration of the Cross. "This is the wood of the Cross on which hung the Savior of the world," intones the priest. "Come let us worship," we respond. The cross is then placed at the entrance to the sanctuary, where the priest venerates it. Any desirous of doing so, walk quietly up and kneel.

The Reproaches are begun: "O my people, what have I done to thee? Or wherein have I wearied thee? Answer me."

"Holy God, Holy and Mighty, Holy and immortal, have mercy upon us."

"We venerate thy Cross, O Lord, and we praise and glorify thy Holy Resurrection; for lo! by the Cross, joy hath come to the whole world."

The sisters sing even more beautifully this year. It is moving to me that they rehearse so long and hard, only that they may sing well for the glory of God. For although anyone is welcome, the community encourages people to attend their own parish churches. Thus an outside congregation is virtually nonexistent.

On Ash Wednesday I spoke of "celebrating" Lent. But I find it impossible to celebrate today as I walk the road to Calvary with Jesus. "A great crowd of people followed him, including the women who beat their breasts and lamented over him" (Lk. 23:26). I am among these, and I hear Jesus say, "Daughters of Jerusalem, do not weep for me, but weep for yourselves and for your children" (Lk. 23:28).

I see my Lord on His grim march to the scaffold, exhausted, staggering under the weight of the cross. I see Him fall into the dust, then painfully rise again to continue His torturous way to be crucified between two thieves. And yet, bent now though He is, weary, begrimed, I never see a defeated man but only the King of Glory.

I hear the taunting mob, "He saved others but he cannot save himself!" (Mt. 27:42). My heart cries out, "You are wrong! Of *course* He could save Himself if He so wished, but were He to do so, He would nullify His life and mission. He knew His appointed end from the very beginning. This is His deliberate act. The Good Shepherd lays down His life for the sheep. 'No one takes it [my life] from me' He said. 'I lay it down freely' " (Jn. 10:18).

Jesus had come to show mankind the love of God. Sent by the Father, He had come to do His will. To save Himself would have been to disobey the dictates of Love, for it was love, not nails, which held Him to the Cross. He never stopped exercising this love on the way to Calvary, nor will He ever.

"Weep not for me, daughters of Jerusalem, but for yourselves." Just now I weep for both.

I come home from the chapel at three o'clock and wander around, aimlessly. I know with my mind that Easter will be here day after tomorrow, but emotionally I am totally depressed. From now until Easter are the most terrible—and the longest—hours of the entire year. I try to pray and cannot. I feel like one of the apostles, confused, bewildered, for my Lord has been crucified. I have the entirely irrational feeling that God is dead. But in my heart I am grateful for this feeling, however irrational I know it to be.

Living these long hours between the crucifixion and the resurrection, I am reminded of what life would be without God.

I think of the Roman centurion standing at the foot of the cross at Calvary, of how his spiritual eyes were gradually opened, so that when it was all over, he would blurt out "Clearly this was the Son of God!" (Mt. 27:54). Each Good Friday that passes, my spiritual eyes, like those of the centurion, seem to open a little wider.

"Were you there when they crucified my Lord? Oh! Sometimes it causes me to tremble."

This question does indeed cause me to tremble, because I know I was.

Father, forgive.

Holy Saturday

This day always seems endless, but the convent schedule shortens it by having the Easter Vigil (except for the Lighting of the Paschal Candle) so early in the evening. In addition to the scriptural readings (the Liturgy of the Word) there is the Renewal of Baptismal Vows. "Through the Paschal mystery . . . we are buried with Christ by Baptism into his death, and raised with him into newness of life." We renew our "vows of Holy Baptism, by which we once renounced Satan and all his works, and promised to serve God faithfully in his holy Catholic Church" (BCP, p. 292).

The admixture of joy and sorrow in this service makes me feel a trifle schizophrenic.

Today in the mail, I found a letter from Father Paul. From his first letter telling me that he was joyfully awaiting his death, Father Paul has granted me the inestimable privilege of sharing in his dying. He writes frequently and today's letter is in response to mine, in which I asked about his thoughts on life after death.

"Going home for Christmas has at least three stages," he writes. "First, the joyful arrival and greetings of loved ones. Secondly, reconciliation: learning to make peace with every single person you may have hurt, *or* who may have hurt you (this could take ages, so we start now). Then at last, the journey into the deeper beauty and silence of love and rapture, companioned (at the beginning at least) by one you love and trust. This is apt to be a real startler!"*

As I read these words I realized how closely they approximated the findings of Dr. Elisabeth Kübler-Ross, well-known for her research in the field of death and dying, as well as other psychiatrists who have joined her in this work. Their general conclusion is that there is definitely life after death.[1] Their evidence is based on the reports of those who have gone through the death process and been resuscitated. Of course the Christian received his "proof" nearly two thousand years ago!

Pondering Father Paul's letter, my mind flew back to a religious conference of several years ago where I was the speaker.

It is the annual one-day conference and very tightly scheduled. I was sitting in the sacristy, grateful to be alone for a few minutes before the evening healing service began. An Episcopal priest walked in, apologized for intruding, and then introduced himself. I looked into his eyes and involuntarily gasped. Then I heard myself say, "You have been with Jesus, haven't you?"

He nodded and said, "I don't know whether you have ever seen anyone who has been raised from the dead." Before I could say anything, the man went on, "You're looking at one now." This, then, explained the look in his eyes.

"I was raised from the dead fifteen years ago," he said. "I had crossed over and my death certificate had already been made out. I was filled with a joy so great I can't even begin to put it into words. Then I heard the most indescribably beautiful voice which said: 'You must go back. Your family needs you desperately.' "

Much as he loved his family, he was completely heartbroken that he could not remain with Jesus. Those moments of so-called death were so wonderful that it took him years to reconcile himself

---

* When Father Paul became blind, he asked me to continue writing which I did. Occasionally one of the friars sent me a card dictated by Father Paul. He was to "go home for Christmas" on December 27, twenty-two months after the diagnosis was made.

to the fact that he had been sent back here, that the conflict within himself after he returned and had to resume life was a battle he thought would never end. After long, long months of prayer, he finally entered the ministry, where he is now deeply involved in healing.

"I have peace now," he said, "but I can hardly wait until I go again to *stay* with our blessed Lord."

Yes, but until then, this priest joyfully lives, celebrates, and seeks to preserve life, which he knows to be God's holy will. The supremely important thing for all of us is, as Paul says, that "Christ will be exalted through me, whether I live or die" (Phil. 1:20); to remember that in Him there is no death, but only life. He has promised that where He is, there shall we be also (Jn. 14:3). This is all we need to know.

Maundy Thursday seems forever ago, but the coming of Easter is now only a matter of hours.

I have always been a "night" person and, by dint of taking an afternoon nap, have continued to remain so despite my early hours here. But tonight I go to bed at a reasonable hour, for tomorrow new life begins at five-fifteen in the morning.

Easter Sunday

Alleluia, Christ is risen: The Lord is risen indeed, Alleluia!

In the darkness the fire is kindled in the back of the chapel, and the voice of the priest breaks into the stillness: "O God, through your Son you have bestowed upon your people the brightness of your light: Sanctify this new fire, and grant that in this Paschal feast we may so burn with heavenly desires, that with pure minds we may attain to the festival of everlasting light" (BCP, p. 285).

The candle, now lighted, is borne down the center aisle. Three stops are made, at each one is sung, "The light of Christ," while we respond, "Thanks be to God." The small candles carried by the sisters and each member of the congregation are lit from the Paschal Candle, which is then placed in its stand in the sanctuary.

By its light the Exsultet is sung, that paschal proclamation which Thomas Merton declared teaches all theology.² And it does, for we are an Easter people living by power of the risen Christ.

"Rejoice now, heavenly host and choirs of angels, and let your trumpets shout Salvation for the victory of our mighty King" (Exsultet, BCP, p. 286).

Finally the candles on the altar are lit and it comes alive in a burst of dazzling brilliance. As the Eucharist is about to begin, I hear in my heart the exultant words, "Christ being raised from the dead will never die again; death no longer has dominion over him. . . . Since by a man came death, by a man has come also the resurrection of the dead. . . . For as in Adam all die, so also in Christ shall all be made alive" (Rom. 6:9; 1Cor. 15:21–22).

Alleluia, Christ is risen. The Lord is risen indeed. Alleluia! And because He has, we need no longer fear death and thus can fully live.

10.

The Precious Blood and Healing

It rained most of last night so I got very little sleep. Most people think of the sound of rain as soothing. So, once, did I, but no longer. There are aluminum awnings over my bedroom windows, and when the rain pelts them it sounds like the rapid fire of machine gun bullets! When it rains all night, it is a continuous barrage. But the night was not a total loss, as I practised what I preach. First, I offered my sleeplessness to God, then prayed for every person and every cause I could think of: all who suffer in any way, all who are alone, all who lie sleepless in hospital beds, all physicians and nurses, the Church, her clergy and people, the nation, the world.

Then I thought of Saint Catherine of Siena whose Feast Day we celebrate today. She had great healing gifts which she used to the full as she worked, as a Dominican Tertiary, among the sick, particularly among lepers and cancer patients.

It is interesting to note that while conservative church people today tend to recoil from such phrases as "Pleading the Blood," Catherine begins a number of her letters, "I write to you in His Precious Blood," and then she bids those to whom she writes to "bathe" or "drown" themselves in the blood of Jesus. In her prayers for others, she frequently speaks of placing them in His blood. Perhaps it was her teaching which led me to pray as I do for certain people, notably leukemia patients (another "new" idea), pleading for a mystical exchange of blood; praying that His blood, whole, perfect, cleansing, redeeming, may flow through their bodies. As I look back and remember her well-known "Dialogue," I may well have had this in my unconscious mind when I began to emphasize the necessity of daily Communion for leukemia victims, regardless of their church affiliation. I can only believe that as a result, many medically incurable cases have been marvelously healed, or in remission for so long that they may be legitimately claimed as "healing."

As women today strive for a place in the sun, I smile to myself at the enormous influence exerted in the Church by a young woman like Catherine who lived in the fourteenth century. She worked tirelessly for the unity of the Church, going to see Pope Gregory XI, and prevailing upon him to return to Rome. Upon his death, when the great papal schism erupted, she deluged cardinals and monarchs with letters, urging them to support Urban VI. She was certainly a great deal more successful in influencing her Church than any one of us who lives in this age of female liberation!

Still practising what I preach, I thanked God when it was time to get up!

Late this morning, Sister Virginia stopped by to tell me she had discovered a lump in her breast and would be entering the hospital in three days. Alas, I shall be far away on mission. We had prayer with the laying on of hands, and I anointed her.

Rushing to the hairdresser, I stepped in a pothole and went sprawling, falling with my full weight on my right hand. But at least I got my hair done for the mission, whence I leave in two days. Tomorrow I have a full day at a local Methodist church, beginning at eight o'clock in the morning, and concluding after the healing service that night.

My hand began to hurt badly while I was under the dryer. Determined to disregard it, I tried to take a nap when I got home, but the pain prevented this. I prayed, got up, and as usual could not remember whether one is supposed to apply heat or cold to an injury of this kind. I did both, to no avail. By seven-thirty, the hand was so badly swollen and discolored, that I called one of the sisters, who is a nurse, to look at it. "Sorry, Emily," she said, "I'm afraid it is broken."

She drove me at once to the emergency room of the nearest hospital, where we spent the next four hours. Saturday night is not the time to go to an emergency room.

Close to midnight, X-rays were at last taken. Shortly thereafter, a doctor came out and said that the hand was fractured, and a small piece of bone had been broken off. He then announced he would put the hand in a cast. I panicked at this news. I had the Methodist church healing service the next night, and was leaving on mission the day after. The healing power goes through my right hand, and in a cast how could I lay on hands? Sister realized the predicament and said she would speak to the doctor and see that the hand was not put in a cast *if* I insisted on keeping my engagements, which she, as a nurse, advised me not to do. I assured her I had led missions with far worse things than a broken hand.

I still have no idea what she told the doctor, but he came out scowling and said, "All right, if you insist, I'll put you in a splint instead." This he proceeded to do, with obvious disapproval.

All the way home from the hospital, Sister tried to dissuade me from doing the work next day. Obviously I could not cancel out at this late date, and she, God bless her, came over next morning at six-thirty to help me dress and put on make-up.

The people at the Methodist church were somewhat startled to see my hand, but the day went well although the hand was very painful. There was a large crowd for the healing service, and precisely when it happened, I don't know. Suddenly, in the middle of the service when I was laying hands on someone, I became aware that my hand so longer hurt. I thanked God and continued. When I looked at my fingers later that evening, all swelling had gone, and there remained no sign of discoloration.

Sister was waiting up for me, and as soon as she saw my light go on, she came over. One look at my hand, and she nearly fainted. She had never seen a healing like this before, and it was to make of her an instant convert to the healing Christ. Fascinated, she had me flex my fingers, and saw that my hand was good as new.

Five days later

It was a good mission though I had trouble keeping my heart in and my mind on it, both of which were with Sister Virginia. My first day there the convent had called me to say that she had just undergone a mastectomy. I wired her flowers and then, with something of a struggle, proceeded to the task at hand.

Often during a mission, one type of healing will seem to predominate. This time, and perhaps not surprisingly, there were a large number of bone healings. Included in these was the healing of a young man's foot and ankle, broken twenty-four hours before. He came to the first healing service in a cast and on crutches. He claimed a healing that night and walked back to his pew without the crutches. He still wore the cast, which he had been unable to break off. He asked me what to do, and I suggested he return to his physician the next day, asking him to X-ray the foot and ankle and then cut off the cast. The young man was at the service the following night to offer thanksgiving. He was minus the cast and was perfectly healed.

That same night, the pastor of the church told me of a twenty-year-old man, David, who had been recently injured in a motorcycle accident. His left leg had been broken very badly and had a twenty-three inch pin in it. I was asked to go to the hospital next day to see him.

Early the next morning I called David so he could prepare himself for our visit. He told me that someone had given him one of my books but he had not quite finished it. He said, apologetically, "I'm in such pain I can't read very fast, but I'll try to finish it before you come." I asked him, instead, to use his strength in praying to the God of all mercy, something like this, but in his own words: "God I love you and I know you love me because you sent your Son to show me how much. Jesus, you lived for me and died and rose from the dead, and you gave your Church the power to heal today, by the Spirit, as you healed when you were on earth. So I know that you can heal my leg. I know that two people who are ministers of your love are coming to see me this afternoon. They want to be open channels for your healing grace and to bring me into a living relationship with you, Jesus."

I asked David to repeat this idea in whatever words he chose to use, three or four times before we came.

When we arrived at the hospital shortly after one o'clock, we found David in severe pain, his broken leg stretched out flat on the bed and his left heel thickly bandaged to prevent its rubbing against the sheet, for his injured limb was an immovable, dead weight.

He was a beautiful youngster and wide-open to the healing touch of Jesus. He was like a sponge, absorbing God. We had the laying on of hands with prayer, and at the end, the love of God having poured itself out upon all three of us, David grinned broadly and said, "You know, I bet I can move this thing," pointing to his leg. Before the pastor or I could say a word, the boy said, "Watch!" with which, up went the leg. Again and again he lifted it, higher and higher and holding it up longer each time. He called in a passing nurse who could hardly believe what she saw, and kept repeating, "It's a miracle!"

The final night of the mission, David's entire family came to offer thanksgiving. The pastor asked the father how long the physician had said it would be before David could move his leg. The answer came loud and clear, "Three months at least." The father went on to say, "We saw David early today when the doctor was with him, and he was flabbergasted. Originally he had said that it would be a full year before the leg was healed. Now he said, 'At this rate, Dave will be walking in less than a month.' "

One of the most moving episodes of the mission, concerned Bill, a former Roman Catholic priest who had left the ministry two years before to marry. As is so frequently the case under such circumstances, Bill was suffering all sorts of emotional upsets due to his inner conflict. He had urgently asked to see me during the mission, so we met one morning alone in the chapel.

He was depressed and withdrawn, one of his chief problems being a crisis of faith and the subsequent loss of any prayer life. After an hour of talk, he asked for prayer and the laying on of hands. During the prayer there occurred that supernatural outpouring of God's love which for me, signifies the actual presence of Jesus and His total reality in our lives. Bill remained kneeling at the altar rail, while I knelt in a front pew. After perhaps ten minutes, he arose and came towards me with outstretched arms, his countenance transfigured with joy as tears streamed down his cheeks. This man, a few minutes before so depressed and withdrawn, now threw his arms around me and kept exclaiming, "He lives and I know it now. He lives and I *know* it!" I said to him, "No more doubts?" and he replied, "No, how could there be? He's *here;* I can *touch* Him! I'll never forget this experience as long as I live."

He was correct: once having tasted God one never completely forgets, though there may well come times when the memory dims. Then the embers of recollection must be rekindled and fanned into flame by the breath of the Holy Spirit and our own desire.

Every mission is different, and yet certain questions never seem to change, among them: "Why do Christians suffer?" Therefore it came as no surprise when this was the first question asked during the discussion period of the mission. My answer as it inevitably must be was: "Why not? We are *all* victims of the evil of this world. The only difference between the pagan and the Christian in regard to suffering is that the Christian knows what to do about it. We turn to the healing Christ in whom we live and move and have our being" (Acts 17:28).

Nevertheless, there seems to lurk in the heart of many Christians the eternal hope that a dedicated Christian need never suffer, but live in a never-never land of sweetness and light. Wherever I go people ask for prayer for those near and dear. Almost invariably the request is preceded by the statement: "He-she is such a wonderful Christian." The inference is clear: such a person should not have to endure pain. However, according to the teaching of Jesus, the sun shines and the rain falls on the evil and good alike (Mt. 5:45). I remember well in my own life, how as soon as I committed my life to Him, not only the roof but the entire sky seemed to fall in!

The last healing of which I was aware occurred at nearly the end of the final service. A man knelt at the altar rail and extended his right hand, the back of which was almost entirely covered by an ugly-looking sore. "Skin cancer," he whispered.

Always when I pray for someone, regardless of the words I

speak, the burden of my heart's prayer is always the same: that the person for whom I pray may have a closer relationship with Jesus, and become a truly new creature in Him. Thus I had begun to pray for this man, lightly covering his cancerous hand with one of my own. Suddenly, in the middle of the prayer he stopped me and said, "I came here for the healing of the skin cancer, but now what I *really* want is to know Jesus as my Savior and Redeemer. I want to know it *here*," and he placed his hand over his heart.

The prayer was offered, and at its end he held up his hand in wonderment for me to see. No sign of the sore remained. The skin was clear and soft as a baby's. He held it up so that everybody could see, as he returned to his pew aglow with the love of Christ. I thought of Naaman cleansed of his leprosy (2 Kings 5:14). I thought also of how once again one of the great truths of the healing ministry had been demonstrated: our willingness to remain *unhealed* physically, if only we may know more of God, greatly increases the likelihood of bodily cure.

For so many during the mission, the light shining out of darkness shone in their hearts, that they might make known the glory of God shining on the face of Christ (2 Cor. 4:6).

I offer Him my grateful heart.

A sister met me at the airport so that we could stop by the hospital to see Sister Virginia before coming home to the convent. I was appalled at how she looked, and hoped my shock was not apparent.

We prayed and I anointed her. (Given permission by my bishop to anoint, I always carry blessed oil in my purse.)

As we embraced before I left, I had an eerie premonition. I cried all the way home.

11.

In the Power of the Spirit

I loitered walking home from mass this morning, savoring this glorious late spring day: bright blue sky, sun shining, flowers blooming, all earth rejoicing in the Ascension of our Lord. My heart sings, "This is the day the Lord has made; let us be glad and rejoice in it" (Ps. 118:24).

Forty days have elapsed since He rose from the dead; the post-Resurrection appearances are over. His human nature now taken into heaven, He exercises all power in heaven and on earth (Mt. 28:18): power to bless, to heal, to sanctify.

The final departure in bodily form of the incarnate God was no matter for sorrow for the disciples, but rather the reverse. They, whose wavering faith had gradually been transformed into a rock-like stability, greeted the Ascension of their Lord with joy and worship. Returning to Jerusalem, they "were to be found in the temple, constantly speaking the praises of God" (Lk. 24:53). They knew now that He reigned, that the power of darkness and evil had been overcome, that death was only the gateway to life.

We today commemorate His Ascension with the same joy as the disciples. We also know that through the Ascension we are all kept in close, continuous, personal contact with the risen, glorified Christ, the Lord of our lives, the Lord on whom all life depends. We know now the glorious fulfillment of His promise, "I am with you always, until the end of the world" (Mt. 28:20). And so He is, blessing, forgiving, pouring out upon us, the fullness of His healing love.

Lord Jesus, you whom I love above and beyond all things, thank

you for your promise that you will never leave us or forsake us
(Jos. 1:5). Again and again I have claimed this promise, and again
and again you fulfill it.

What can I offer *You?* Alas, nothing but myself—all that I have,
all that I am—asking You to use me according to your holy purpose, where you will, how you will, and with whom you will.
(You see, Lord, no matter how hard I try, I invariably ask you for
something, even if it is to use me.)

Sister Virginia came home from the hospital about a week ago.
After mass the following morning, the chaplain had left the oratory carrying the Sacrament, preceded as always by the sacring
bell, rung by one of the sisters. I hoped the Sacrament was for Sister Virginia, and it was. When the chaplain emerged from her
room in the infirmary, I slipped in for a minute to see her. She
looks wonderful. It must have been my own fatigue after the mission and the seven-hour trip home, that was responsible for the
"premonition" I thought I had felt that night in the hospital.

Pentecost

Ten days ago we celebrated our Lord's Ascension which was
the signal, so to speak, for the coming of the Holy Spirit upon His
Church, bringing to it knowledge and power and strength, leading
us into all truth.

Ever since the Ascension, His disciples, both men and women
(including His Mother) have been gathered in the Upper Room
eagerly and expectantly awaiting the coming of the Holy Spirit
which Jesus promised, the Spirit, "whom the Father will send in
my name, [who] will instruct you in everything, and remind you
of all that I told you" (Jn. 14:26).

The Holy Spirit has come, the third Person of the Trinity, God
at work in our lives today. And now we are endued with power
from on high.

Two thousand years ago He came upon that group of believers

who were to be His Church, which is why Pentecost is known as the birthday of the Church. All those believers were together in one accord and in one place, as Jesus had instructed them, awaiting the Spirit. He came, and when He descended, He came also to us, for it is as Peter said, "You must reform and be baptized, each one of you, in the name of Jesus Christ, that your sins may be forgiven; then you will receive the gift of the Holy Spirit. It was to you and to your children that the promise was made, and to all those still far off" (Acts 2:38–39). And this means you and me today and all the generations yet to come.

To be sure, we all received the Holy Spirit at the time of our baptism, but unless we appropriate Him we are little different than the pagans (despite Saint Augustine's assertion that by their baptism, Christians will be recognized even in hell!).

For those who are baptized as infants or young children or later, perhaps, as mere ritual, this appropriation will take the form of conscious, personal commitment to Jesus, who is central to the faith: He exercises His lordship through the Holy Spirit.

Appropriation of the Spirit is never a once-and-for-all experience. As Christians we pray throughout our lives for more and more of Him, that He may continually increase in us until we come into God's everlasting kingdom. In response to prayer, there are frequent infillings of Him, so that whatever our task, He strengthens and empowers us to perform it in Jesus' name.

How well I know this! Just one small example: I had studied to be a concert violinist, and at the age of sixteen had begun, in a small way, to concertize. A year later I stopped because I could not endure the stage fright I suffered each time I played in public. My marriage, at a young age, happily and permanently removed me from any further consideration of the concert stage. Furthermore, until I became a Christian, I was careful never to get myself into a situation which would require me to speak in public. In short, doing anything before an audience terrified me and rendered me both helpless and speechless.

I think on these things occasionally, when on mission, I look out over the vast congregation to whom I am about to speak. I smile to myself, as in the power of the Spirit, I begin.

Musing on the events which occurred in the Upper Room, reminds me that last Monday night at the healing service at Saint Thomas, I spoke on the widely used nine days of prayer, which has as its origin those nine days during which the assembled believers awaited the coming of the Holy Spirit. I have found this method extremely efficacious in praying for the sick. At the end of that evening at Saint Thomas a number of the congregation asked me questions, then gathered together and decided to engage in a novena.

In seeking a special grace, this form of prayer is traditionally addressed, for each of the nine days, either to the Holy Spirit invoking His power, or to the Holy Mother asking her intercession.

Yesterday I found a message at the convent from one of those at Saint Thomas who, for the first time, was engaged in the nine days of prayer. The mother of a small child who was very ill, she left word that she was asking the intercession of the Blessed Mother. She wrote, "As a mother who had suffered over her Son, I, as a suffering mother also, have a deep feeling of kinship with her. I know how well she understands." Yesterday was the sixth day of the novena and she reported her child greatly improved.

Yes. "Remember, O most loving Virgin Mary, that never was it known that any who fled to thy protection, implored thy help, and sought thy intercession, was left unaided" (Saint Bernard).

The telephone was ringing when I got home from the festive mass this morning. The call was from a woman telling me that she had been gravely injured in an automobile accident, and asking for prayer. After we had hung up, my mind went back to another morning, some time ago.

I had just put on the water for coffee when the telephone rang. It was a long distance call from a woman of whom I had never heard. As I caught the hysteria in her voice, I must confess my first reaction was, "Oh, dear. If only I had had a chance to drink that coffee I could handle this better."

She was crying uncontrollably, so it was difficult to decipher her story but I finally understood. She was in another city, her husband, in a hospital, was dying of cancer. She had no family; the two of them were alone in the world. If he died she simply could not endure it, and would I please come to see him quickly.

I asked her how she had got my unlisted telephone number, and she replied that I had given it to her at a mission I was leading. That must have been a very long time ago, before I realized that if people had my number I would have no time to eat or sleep.

I told this poor, distraught soul how sorry I was about her husband and assured her that we would pray for him here. I expressed my honest regret that I could not possibly go to see him, explaining that if I acceded to all who asked, I would never be out of a plane. I also told her that I have no magic to offer. Prayer has no geographical boundaries, and others who live in the locality of the sick can administer the healing rites.

This good woman must have been familiar with the parable of the Friend at Midnight (Lk. 11:5-8) and hence with the effectiveness of perseverance. She called me every ten minutes all day long. About nine o'clock that night she delivered the coup de grace: she put her husband on the line. When I heard his weak, pleading voice, I agreed, against my better judgment, to fly from Cincinnati the next day at noon, returning on a three o'clock plane. This would give me only ten or fifteen minutes with the sick man, but it was the best I could do. The rest I left in God's hands.

Next day my plane left promptly and thanks be to God arrived on time, despite a severe thunderstorm at my destination. The Lord must have had His hand on the traffic lights going from the airport to the hospital. We got there so quickly that I had nearly half an hour to spend with the dying man.

By the time I arrived at the hospital, he was unable to speak, but I could see by his eyes that he understood what I was trying to tell him of the love of God.

The presence of Christ in that hospital was palpable. Once again it was as if I could actually see the hand of God mold the spirit of the sick man and, even more remarkable, that of his distraught wife. At the end of the brief healing service, both husband and wife were radiant. The man, who a few minutes before could not speak, said to me in a strong, clear voice, "Now I *know* that I am healed." Then he said those words which never fail to gladden my heart, "Nothing seems to matter now, except that this afternoon I have known Jesus. I have experienced His love and His mercy, and I know that I am whole."

I was ten minutes later than I had intended in leaving for the airport, but again, God had His hand on lights and traffic and I made my plane home.

I had seen the healing Christ at work that afternoon. The extent of my disobedience had I failed to go, makes me tremble. Those two people had an unparalleled experience of God in a small hospital room.

Three days later the wife was to call me, and in a calm, sweet voice thank me for bringing God to her and her husband. He had died a few hours before, a quiet, pain-free, and holy death. She, who was totally hysterical three days before, was now strong in the Lord. This is the power of God.

Later she took over and officially conducted her husband's business. Moreover, she joined a healing prayer group in an Episcopal church (she and her husband were Baptists). Each week she prayed for, and received the healing rite on behalf of, others. She loved the rector of that church, and when he, whose health had long been poor, died suddenly, her faith in the healing Christ remained undaunted.

A short while after this, I was scheduled to lead a mission to which she was looking forward with great joy. Two days before the mission, I injured by back and had to cancel. Fortunately I was able to send a wonderful and gifted Methodist minister in my stead. I tried hard to reach her to tell her what had happened, but was unsuccessful. Knowing that she had chartered a bus to bring people from her home town over three hundred miles away, I was worried.

After the mission was over, I received a letter from her and if I had ever had any doubts as to her wholeness, they would now have been dispelled.

She wrote, "I was crushed, and so were all the others, when I discovered you weren't there to lead the mission. But I remembered what you taught: that it wasn't *you* who did anything, it was God and God alone. I told all my friends this, and we received tremendous benefit from the mission."

And now, today, the call telling me of her accident and the terrible injuries she had received. Through all her trials, not once has she said or written, "Why me?"; only, "I am so grateful I know Jesus. He is always with me, and through Him, I have dominion over pain." Her faith and her conviction of His love has never wavered.

I thank God for her, for how He has transfigured her life despite tragedy, for the wonderful witness she is to Him.

Both she and her husband came to know the living Christ before the latter died. Now he knows the glory of the kingdom fulfilled. She has glimpsed the glory, perhaps the more clearly because her eyes have been tear-filled.

The wonder of it all never ceases for me, nor my gratitude to the Holy and undivided Trinity for bringing it to pass.

"Keep watch, dear Lord, with those who work, or watch, or weep this night, and give your angels charge over those who sleep. Tend the sick, Lord Christ; give rest to the weary, bless the dying, soothe the suffering, pity the afflicted, shield the joyous; and all for your love's sake" (attributed to Saint Augustine; BCP, p. 134).

And now it is late and once again I must pack as I go on mission early tomorrow morning.

12.

God in Small Things

June 11
Saint Barnabas the Apostle

It is a great joy to walk into my apartment after a trip away, for there are always "welcome home" notes inside the door, and depending on the time of year, fresh flowers galore adorn my living room. In season and out, there is invariably a single perfect rose. One of the sisters procures three roses each week: one for the Holy Mother, one for the Mother Superior, and one for me. I am in good company! After the last mission there was a large card on the table reading, "Joy is when Emily comes home!" Bless the sisters who do all this.

I am afraid I turned out to be more nuisance than joy this time. Three days after getting home, I came down with an acute attack of bronchitis. The sisters were in silent retreat and I had no intention of letting them know. However, when I was not at mass they knew something was wrong and one of them came over to investigate. Having lived alone for a long while, I am accustomed to fending for myself. Therefore it has been a great treat to experience the care and love shown me by the sisters. Unasked and certainly unexpected, one of them brought over my dinner each night; another came and sat silently beside me for a few minutes, while yet another quietly arranged fresh flowers. All of this made me wonder anew why more of our parish churches do not do this sort of thing for their members.

During the few days I was laid up, I had time to do a lot of thinking. I thought about the last mission, beginning with the trip there. I had been exuberant because I was booked on a through flight to the South with no change of planes in Atlanta. The saying is that to get to heaven one must go via Atlanta. I would think this very likely, adding that this midway point would automatically take care of the purgatory stopover.

My last mishap at Atlanta occurred several years ago. The airport was iced in and closed for twenty-four hours immediately after my plane landed. It was impossible to get food or even a cup of coffee. After this experience I vowed never again to accept a mission which would necessitate going through Atlanta. Hence my delight at discovering that there was one through plane going where I was bound this time.

Two weeks prior to my departure, the airline took off the through plane, and once again, Atlanta loomed. We were due at eleven-thirty in the morning. At precisely that moment the pilot announced: "Ladies and gentlemen, we apologize. It looks as if we cannot land in Atlanta, so we will go on to Birmingham. Planes are banked up over the airport. There is only one runway open, and we have only enough fuel to circle until noon. On the one chance in a million that we can land, we will continue to circle a few minutes longer."

I instantly asked the stewardess how I could get out of Birmingham in order to reach my destination. Her reply was short and discouraging: fly back to Atlanta and get a plane to where I was going. I envisioned myself missing the mission as I tried for the next three days to get back to Atlanta and out again. As it was close to twelve o'clock, I began the noon office: "O God make *speed* to save us; O Lord make *haste* to help us." Just then came the pilot's voice: "I am happy to say that we are about to begin our descent to Atlanta." The connecting plane had also been delayed, so the connection was made. That was the first miracle of the mission though by no means the last. (I am sure God must honor my travel prayer. I have prayed it so often, and however dim the prospects, have never missed a connection.)

The mission was sponsored by a Lutheran church, but the evening services were held in a Baptist church, whose pastor had kindly granted us its use, as it was the largest church in town. I was pleased that he came to all the services, and on the last night asked if he might participate in the laying on of hands. Of course we were delighted, and when he said to me afterwards, "This has been one of the great experiences of my ministry. Thank you for giving it to me," my cup of happiness was full.

Some truly spectacular healings occurred, healings bearing on every area of life. However, wonderful as these healings always are, it is even more wonderful to me to see and recognize the hand of God in all the small things which happen to all of us continually. Last Monday night I spoke of this at Saint Thomas, and afterwards a number of people said exactly the same thing, just in slightly different words: "I've been so busy looking for the 'spectacular' that I wasn't even aware of how God has been working in me in countless small ways. Suddenly, tonight, I realize that I am healed."

Remarks like this gladden my heart, because until we are able to see God in everything good, His action in all things no matter how miniscule, we are not habitually aware of His presence. It is never a question of "coming into" His presence at particular times, we are already, and continually, in it.

It is the small things which, to me, most poignantly signify His personal interest and love for each one of us. We speak much of miracles in the healing Church, of sick bodies cured, of ailing spirits renewed, of broken relationships mended. Yet I think we do not speak often enough of what is, in a very real sense, the greatest of all miracles: that we are permitted to communicate with Almighty God, Creator of heaven and earth, Ruler of the universe; and that He, who guides the stars in their courses, hears and cares.

The other day, for example, I lost the cross which I have worn ever since I began to work in the healing ministry. This Jerusalem or crusader cross has all sorts of meaning for me, among them the fact that many who have regained their sight have seen its shine as the first evidence of their restored vision. When I realized it was gone I panicked and began a frantic search. Then I came to my senses and sat quietly down, asking Jesus where it was. I sat for perhaps ten minutes, and then came the direction clearly imprinted on my heart: "Look in the wardrobe." What on earth would it be doing there? But I began to look. The problem was I did not know where in the wardrobe to search. I was about to close the door when I found myself going through some sweaters hanging there. For no good human reason, I thrust my hand down the sleeve of one, and there was the cross! I realized then what must have happened: I had worn that sweater to mass early in the morning when it was chilly. In taking it off, evidently the chain had got tangled in the wool of the sleeve as I pulled it over my head. Such a little thing, but very important to me.

Afterward, I pondered on how, two thousand years ago, Philip had said to Jesus, "Lord, show us the Father." And Jesus had replied, "Philip, after I have been with you all this time, you still do not know me?" (Jn. 14:8, 9). Of course what Philip wanted and expected to see when he said "Show us the Father" was a flaming sign, a great glory, a dazzling splendor. Instead of that, Jesus told him that in his daily life for all the three years Philip had been with Him, he had been seeing the Father. And so it is with us. As we progress in the life of the spirit, we see the glory of God in the face of Jesus Christ not only in great signs and wonders and dramatic healings but in *all* things that are good. We find our Lord who knows the number of hairs on each of our heads, not only in the majesty of mountains or in the mighty seas or the vast expanse of interstellar space, but most intimately in the still, small voice.

Yesterday I counselled as usual at Saint Thomas, and was so happy to see the great improvement of a young man who has been coming to me for months, suffering from agoraphobia, a phobic state in which anxiety is aroused when the patient tries to leave his familiar home environment, until eventually he may be unable to leave home at all. My counselee had reached the latter state, totally unable to leave his house even when armed with the massive doses of Valium prescribed by his psychiatrist. A friend drove him to see me each week. The road back to health has been long and tortuous. Coming in to see me every week was for a long time, absolute agony for him, but he is now virtually well, thanks be to God.

I had him begin by walking into a store and walking straight out again. This he did for weeks, only with the help of prayer and Valium. When he could do this without the Valium, I had him make a single purchase, very near the front of the store. Then came making his purchase further back in the store, until at last he was able to purchase a long grocery list and stand at the check-out counter. Eventually he could go to a restaurant, ordering first only a cup of coffee, until finally he managed to order a meal and sit and eat it. Then came the great day of victory, when he drove himself in to see me—all without any medication.

He is a Roman Catholic, long unable to go to mass, and he was embarrassed to begin by walking into the church and then straight out. With his permission, I talked to his priest and explained the situation. My counselee sat for many weeks in the very last pew on the aisle so he could get out quickly without disturbing anyone. He has now been going to mass every Sunday for a number of weeks, and has made two confessions.

Yesterday I prayed for him and anointed him again. Two or three more sessions and I shall be able to dismiss him, healed. We praised God together and offered Him our grateful hearts.

Barnabas, whose feast we celebrate today, means "son of comfort, the encourager"—surely a fitting name for this apostle and companion of Saint Paul.

"Grant, O God, that we may follow the example of your faithful servant, Barnabas, who, seeking not his own renown but the well-being of your Church, gave generously of his life and substance for the relief of the poor and the spread of the Gospel" (BCP, p. 241).

This sums up pretty accurately what we attempt to do in and through the healing ministry of the Church.

13.

The Bread of Life

Thursday after Trinity Sunday
Corpus Christi

How glad I am to be home and not on mission on this glorious day! It is, for me, one of the most meaningful of all the feasts, as it commemorates the institution of the Holy Eucharist.

I used to wonder why this gift was not commemorated on the Thursday in Holy Week when our Lord actually instituted it. Then I realized that the memory of His passion made necessary a separate feast day. I smile to myself as I note that it was Blessed Juliana, a nun of the thirteenth century who took action in this matter. By the fourteenth century, the celebration of this feast on this particular day was universal in the Western Church.

Pope John XXIII remarked that even *hearing* (and I have found even *speaking*) about the Eucharist confers a blessing.[1] However, I smile in recollection of this day several years ago, when it seemed a *mixed* blessing. I had been asked to speak on the sacrament, and at the conclusion of the service it appeared to me that the entire church surged back to say in accusatory tones, "I drove miles to come to hear you speak on *healing*, and instead you speak on this!" This was one of the times when I had obviously spoken in vain.

The Eucharist is a holy mystery. No one really understands its full meaning. However, its transforming power we know well. It is the sacrament of wholeness, and the greatest of all healing services. It is my conviction that no one who has the remotest idea of what he is doing, can receive the body and blood of Christ and remain unchanged. In this sacrament we receive *Him,* His very life, in whom lies all wholeness of body, mind, and spirit.

Many churches regard Holy Communion as merely a memorial: "Do this *in remembrance* of me." One difficulty lies in the translation of the Greek word *anamnesis* which evidently cannot be precisely translated in English. It has the sense of recalling, a reenactment, a *presently* operative effect of an event.[2] Thus, "Do this in remembrance of me," does not imply a looking back into the past, but rather the bringing of the past into the present. The Mass, the Eucharist, the Lord's Supper, whatever one chooses to call it, is then a continuing representation of his self-offering. It was once and for all, yes (Heb. 10:10); yet it is a continual reenactment of His sacrifice. It is at once the great corporate act of worship of the Church, and at the same time, it is for me, the supreme unitive experience of God.

Is my concept of the Eucharist a blind acceptance of the teaching of my Church? No, I believe it to be firmly based on Scripture and the teaching of the primitive Church. "I am the bread of life," He said, "'if anyone eats this bread he shall live forever; the bread I will give is my flesh, for the life of the world" (Jn. 6:48, 51). We say, as did the Jews of that day, "How can he give us his flesh to eat?" Thereupon Jesus said to them, and to us, "If you do not eat the flesh of the Son of Man and drink his blood, you have no life in you" (Jn. 6:52, 53).

I do not understand this, but I know it is true. Because this sacrament is life for me, I moved here to the convent where I could be assured daily Communion. This is why I get up at what, for me, is the middle of the night: to receive His body and blood. I do not regard this as an obligation, but rather as a privilege. Never is there a morning that I do not waken in joyous anticipation of meeting my Lord in this way at the altar rail. All of which is not to say that I do not look forward to the late mass on Tuesday mornings. It is an incredible luxury to sleep in on these days, and walk over to the convent in broad daylight instead of in the pitch black of early morning!

Obviously those who hold a different view of Holy Communion are not denied healing. God is in no way bound by the sacraments, although I undoubtedly am! (However, I note with interest that many nonsacramental churches which are presently engaged in the healing ministry, have greatly increased the number of their celebrations.)

Regardless of the teaching of any one branch of the Church, there is grace received through the sacrament, and many have shared my discovery that one of the most powerful means of intercession is to receive the sacrament with special intention for either an individual in need or a cause. We pray something like this: "Lord, I receive today with special intention for *N.*, praying that the benefits you won for us at Calvary may be especially bestowed upon *N.* through this particular Eucharist."

"Grant us, O Lord, so to venerate the sacred mysteries of your Body and Blood, that we may perceive within ourselves [and those for whom we pray] the fruit of your redemption" (BCP, p.252, paraphrase).

If you are unable, for reasons beyond your control, to receive Holy Communion as often as you would like, you may if you so desire, make a spiritual communion. At whatever time of day or night you do this, you will know that at that moment there will be churches somewhere in the world offering the Eucharist at their altars. Thus, in union with the faithful, offer Him your sacrifice of praise and thanksgiving, seek the forgiveness of your sins, and in an act of oblation, pray, "Lord Jesus, I unite myself to your perpetual, unceasing, universal sacrifice. I offer myself to You every day of my life and every moment of every day (Saint Therese Couderc)."

May the body and blood of our Lord Jesus Christ preserve my body and soul unto everlasting life.

Just the other day at Saint Thomas, I remarked to someone that the Eucharist is the greatest of healing services. "Why, then," came the reasonable question, "do we need specific healing services?" The answer: simply because we attempt to follow, as best we can, the teaching of our Lord. In His earthly ministry He differentiated between preaching the Gospel and healing the sick. In other words, healing was a specific ministry. He commissioned His Church to preach, to teach, to heal, and to "do this in remembrance of me." The Eucharist is the great sacrament of consummation, as it was known in the ancient Church. It is the climax, the seal, of all healing. The body of Christ, the bread of heaven; the blood of Christ, the cup of salvation.

There is a tendency for those who feel they have the gift of healing, to chafe under the restraints of the Church. Finally, in their impatience, they begin to work alone. When this is done, abuses in the healing ministry occur.

I still remember how appalled I was when, at a mission, a woman stood up during the discussion period and announced that her pastor refused to hold healing services. "*I* believe in the healing ministry," she said, "and so do several of my friends. So *we're* going to start healing services." Involuntarily I exploded, "But you can't do that!" Her response was, "Why not? *You* do." I most certainly do not. I have always worked under the authority of my Church, and know too well that to do otherwise is to court disaster. I recall the "teams" of people who worked alone in Pittsburgh, having left their church. I remember the terrible damage they did as they walked through hospitals, unasked and unwanted, telling patients that if they had enough faith they would leave the hospital and go home. I recall the several lives tragically lost because they followed this dubious "advice"; and the guilt of others who did not, but felt their faith was wanting.

I think now of how I have pled with those whom I believed truly had the gift of healing to be patient and wait. I think with joy and thanksgiving of one friend who has the gift of healing. She waited for fifteen years before she began publicly to exercise this gift. You may say, "Fifteen wasted years because she waited for her church to authorize her work." Not so. The years were not wasted. They were a period of spiritual growth, of steadily increasing knowledge and wisdom. My patient friend could pray, and pray she did. The gifts of the Spirit, of which healing is one, are not the private possession of any single individual. They are given to build up the Church, and ultimately they belong *to* the Church.

I reflect on the Church and what it is. Today it is defined almost exclusively as the people of God. However, it is much more. It is the Mystical Body of which Christ is the Head. It is an institution, fallible and flawed because it is run by imperfect men and women. It is a hospital for sinners, which should answer those who refuse to go to church because it is "filled with hypocrites." Rather it is filled with sinners, most of whom know their need for forgiveness. And at the same time, and this is what we tend to overlook today, the Church is the bride of Christ (Rev. 21:2), "holy and immaculate, without stain or wrinkle" (Eph. 5:27).

Ignatius and others of his time, saw the Church as a whole, not so much as *representing* Christ, but as being Christ on earth. The primitive Church "prayed in the person of Christ,"[3] which may well explain its spiritual dynamism as compared to the Church today. If we believe in the Church as the bride of Christ, it is not difficult to conceive of the Church as one with Him (Eph. 5:24–31). As Henri Nouwen states, "The Church through its liturgical life is the ongoing representation of the living Christ in our time and our place."[4] This is another way of expressing the theological truth that the Church is the extension of the Incarnation.

I pray now, as I do every day of my life: "Gracious Father, we pray for thy holy Catholic Church. Fill it with all truth, in all truth with all peace. Where it is corrupt, purify it; where it is in error, direct it; where in any thing it is amiss, reform it. Where it is right, strengthen it; where it is in want, provide for it; where it is divided, reunite it; for the sake of Jesus Christ thy Son our Savior" (BCP, p. 816).

I have just read my mail, and in it is a letter from a man who writes, "I don't need the Church. The Holy Spirit is more abundantly manifested in my living room than in any church." He concludes by saying, "Nevertheless, I am a good Christian."

Why did he write me? Because he was in trouble and needed the ministration of the Church. The sentiments he expresses in his letter, are true of many. It is due to a misunderstanding of the faith, which teaches that no one can be a Christian *alone*. From the earliest times, the disciples risked their lives to meet together in corporate worship and in the breaking of bread. *They* were the Church in those days. To be a Christian is to be a member of the Body of Christ, the community of the faithful, the Church, for "Christ gave Himself up for her to make her holy" (Eph. 5:26). The primacy of the individual at the expense of the Body is contrary to the teaching of Scripture. As Paul says, "None of us lives to himself, and none of us dies to himself" (Rom. 14:7).

To be obedient to Scripture and to Jesus Christ, we must accept "the discipline of the liturgical life of the Church, the Bible, and our own hearts."[5] No one of these things is, of itself, enough. All three are necessary.

I reflect on the healing ministry: surely one of the great values of healing services lies in the fact that all of these conditions are met. Moreover, those in attendance are representatives of the Body, the Church, which accounts for the power manifested in such services. He does not fail to hear the prayers of our hearts: "Regard not our sins, O Lord, but the faith of your Church."

Last Sunday, I spoke in a local church. After the service we went to the parish hall for coffee, after which came the question period. I think this afternoon of the attractive young woman and her husband, members of a nonsacramental church, who rather belligerently proclaimed, "We're born-again Christians. We don't need all this extraneous stuff like the laying-on-of-hands and anointing. Why do you make such a point of these things?" Then the woman added, "Don't you believe in *prayer?*"

Again I saw the all too common misunderstanding, that the sacraments and prayer are mutually exclusive. No sacrament or sacramental rite is magic: without prayer they are powerless gimmicks and empty symbols. But they are never used without prayer. As to why we use the sacramental healing rites, my answer was simple. Our Lord did.

He used many different methods of healing but most often used *acts* accompanied by *word.* He laid hands on the sick (Mk. 6:15). He touched the eyes of the blind (Mt. 9:29). He anointed with clay and spittle (Jn. 9:6). He put His fingers into deaf ears and touched mute tongues (Mk. 7:33). All of these are sacramental acts.

Humanity lives in a sacramental world. The kiss, the handshake, the pat on the head are all outward and visible signs of an inward intention. Our Lord knew the value of *acts* in healing, as so many psychologists today recognize the value of ritual. The danger comes if we worship the ritual instead of God. Occasionally this happens, but not if we are on guard against it. We do not throw out the baby with the bath water by casting aside all ritual because a few may abuse it, nor do we abandon the sacraments because the uninformed may mistake them for magic.

It is as Simon Tugwell says: "Love must use signs. . . . We must be formed by something that expresses for us the mystery of God and the mystery of His love. . . . And surely this is precisely what the sacraments . . . the whole ritual structure of the church, in fact, is intended to provide for us."[6]

Lord Jesus, You who are the bread of life, evermore give us this bread that You may live in us and we in You.

After Compline

Tonight, my Lord, the lifting up of my hands shall be my evening sacrifice. "I will bless the Lord at all times; his praise shall be ever in my mouth" (Ps. 34:1).

And now to bed, where I shall lie down in peace, to fall asleep at once (paraphrase of Ps. 4:8).

14.

"Trust in Him and He Will Act"

June 28
Irenaeus

The weather this entire month has been hot and humid, favorable for the tornadoes which occasionally beset this part of the country. Thank God for air-conditioners! My apartment is comfortable, and the oratory positively chilly. I observe that we are all doing a lot more praying in there than usual.

Last evening was a "first" for me. As I stepped out my back door on the way to Compline, I noticed a curious yellowish light bathing the convent grounds. Glancing at the sky, I saw a distinctly funnel-shaped cloud. "So *that's* what a tornado looks like," I thought to myself, feeling like Dorothy in the Wizard of Oz.

For reasons known only to God, weather constitutes a challenge to me, and the more inclement the greater the challenge. So instead of sensibly returning home and turning on my weather radio, I made a dash for the convent. No sooner had I entered the oratory, when the order came from the Mother Superior to retreat to the basement because of a tornado warning. Down we all trooped and there we stayed and *stayed* and *stayed*. Thinking of all I had to do at home, I grew increasingly restless and wanted to leave. Permission refused. One of the sisters passed around a box of candy which helped somewhat, until, at long last, the warning was lifted. (The tornado passed us by, though it struck close by and caused much damage.) If forced to choose between the two, I prefer hurricanes which are more predictable!

Irenaeus, whom we remember today, was one of the early Church Fathers. He is known as the first Catholic theologian and is accepted by Catholics and Protestants alike as the undivided Church's first systematic theologian. This morning after mass, I re-read portions of his well-known treatise, "Against Heresies." It reminds me that since the beginning of the Church there have been heresies to fight. Throughout the New Testament we are cautioned against false doctrine, and with today's turmoil within the Church it is vaguely comforting to realize that we are not undergoing anything new (even the heresies are not new).

I recall this morning's prayer for Irenaeus: "Almighty God, you upheld your servant Irenaeus with strength to maintain the truth against every blast of vain doctrine: Keep us, we pray, steadfast in your true religion."[1] Yes, only in the true faith once and for all delivered (Jude 3) is there to be found the power of the resurrected Christ.

I particularly like the emphasis of Irenaeus on Scripture and the traditional elements of the Church, insofar as they existed in the early third century.

I also like what he says (and for that matter, all the patristic Fathers of the ante-Nicene Church) concerning healing in the Church. He speaks at length of driving out demons, the healing of many through the laying on of hands, and cites cases of the raising of the dead. "Those who are in truth His disciples," he says, "receiving grace from Him, perform miracles. For as she [the Church] has received freely from God, freely also does she minister to others."

Afternoon

Once again, the mercy of God in having so fresh in my memory the writings of Irenaeus. At noon I found in my mail a letter from one of my daughters.

She had written me previously that, while on vacation with her husband, she had picked up a flu "bug" which seemed determined to stay with her. The letter I now held in my hand told me that she had suffered what seemed to be a sharp recurrence of the infection. Her physician examined her carefully, performed a number of tests, and made his diagnosis. She did not have flu at all, but rather a medically incurable, crippling disease.

She was, as always, optimistic and courageous. For hours, to my shame, I was neither. In short, I fell apart. Like any mother, what happened to me was unimportant; but to one of my children? Ah, that was a different story. All I could envision was the scores of people I had seen at missions suffering the same disease: horribly crippled, in wheelchairs, all suffering agony. Some were healed and others not.

Sister Virginia happened to stop by and found me in tears, the letter still in my hand. This time, *she* did the praying.

It was my day off, so I spent the rest of the afternoon reading Scripture and praying.

I have hidden your word in my heart, O Lord, and within my heart I treasure all your promises (Ps. 119:11).

I praise you, O God, that you are and that I know it. I thank you for my child's life, and my knowledge of your love and healing power.

"Stand firm in the faith, be courageous, be strong" (1 Cor. 16:13). Yes, Lord, but let your merciful kindness be upon her, as I put my trust in you.

Lord God, indeed I know that your favors are not exhausted nor your mercies spent, so great is your faithfulness (Lam. 3:22–24). This knowledge sustains me and forever will, but just for now I have to fight down fear for my child.

Help me, Lord Jesus, to focus my heart and mind on you. By your wounds, we were healed (1 Pet. 2:24), and so will she be. You came that we might have life and have it more abundantly (Jn. 10:10), and for her as for everyone, your perfect will is for life and for wholeness, abundant and overflowing. By your sacrifice, she *is* saved and made every whit whole. Keep me close to you, my Lord: let me not stray into the paths of apprehension. In you I put my trust, now and forever.

Thank you, Lord Jesus, that I know you are so near. How closely today I identify with the suffering of your Blessed Mother.

Thank you, too, that I know you have no joy in afflicting or griev-
ing your children (Lam. 3:33). No one knows better than I, O
Lord, and few as well, that with you all things are indeed possible.
Now I commit to you for blessing, healing, and strengthening, my
beloved child. Thank you, Lord Jesus, and to you be the praise and
the glory forever.

Night

Tomorrow I am speaking to a group on intercessory prayer for
healing. Again, the timing is the mercy of God, as my heart is necessarily centered where it should be: on Him to whom we pray. I
gather my thoughts together now, hoping that the end result will
help others just as preparing what I want to say is helping me.

Praying for others is often referred to as the "work of intercession," and work it is, for it requires time, discipline, effort, and a
great deal of love for God and His children. Work though intercession may be, it is above and beyond all else a labor of love.

I think it important to remember that there is no magic incanta-
tion of certain words which will guarantee healing results precisely when and how we might wish them to occur. It is not words
but the attitude behind them which is important. No two of us
pray in the same way. Each of us has a certain attraction to a particular kind of prayer. We learn all that we can of prayer by *doing*,
not merely reading. Then we ask the Spirit not only to guide us
but to pray in us. The prayer which emerges is what is most natural to us.

Another thing to remember: God knows the need, and we don't
have to spend hours explaining it to Him!

Someone during the last mission asked why, if God knows the
need, we must pray at all. Simply because He tells us to: "He told
them a parable on the necessity of praying always, and not losing
heart" (Lk. 18:1).

We follow as best we can the example of our Lord. We remember how He prayed for Peter that his faith might not fail (Lk.
22:32), for those who caused His agony, and most of all we remember His passionate intercession in the great high priestly

prayer of the seventeenth chapter of John. I read this prayer again and again, seeing in it all the elements of perfect intercession: faith, compassion, love, total consecration.

Paul continually assures his converts that he prays and makes requests to God for them. "Present your needs to God in every form of prayer and in petitions full of gratitude" (Phil. 4:6). Thus we pray *explicitly*—but for our sakes, not God's!

Christ lives to make intercession for us (Heb. 7:25). Therefore, every Christian being in Christ and Christ in him is caught up in the great work of interceding. We are fellow-workers with God, which seems to me an awesome privilege. He uses us as His instruments, and He who has commanded us to pray has willed that the increase He gives should come about through our prayers.

In order that we may be effective instruments, the first step in intercession is to offer ourselves to Him for preparation. Toward that end, we pray that the Holy Spirit may increase in us, that He may strengthen our faith and increase our love. We pray to Him for the forgiveness of our sins, both known and unknown, for we are told that the "fervent petition of a holy man is powerful indeed" (Jas. 5:16). We are called to be holy, but I suspect that for those like me, our "holiness" must consist largely of our holy desire. But thanks be to God, He honors even the *desire*!

As our sins of the spirit, such as resentment, jealousy, and envy impede the inflow of God's healing power within us, so may these same spiritual sins, if unconfessed, diminish the effectiveness of our prayers for others. I believe one of the most serious hindrances to efficacious prayer, whether for ourselves or others, lies in our failure to forgive those who have hurt us. So we pray that God may help us to forgive as He has already forgiven. It is His absolution which cleanses and makes us open channels and powerful conveyors of His grace.

We praise Him in whom we live and move and have our being. We worship Him in spirit and in truth. We offer Him thanksgiving for so much, above all for Himself. We offer Him our grateful hearts that He lives and that we know it, that He hears all prayer however inadequate. We proffer Him ourselves, our souls and bodies, praying that He will use us as His instruments. And then we begin to intercede, or to pray for ourselves.

There are so many ways to do this. Among the simplest: we bring those for whom we pray, one by one and each by name, before God. Their hands in ours, standing together in the divine light, we give praise and thanksgiving for their lives, asking that they be made every whit whole, all brokenness mended, according to His most perfect will.

Or we pray that He may empty us of all desire, except that His holy will may be done. Quietly and without harassment, we wait upon Him, bringing each soul to Jesus, resting with them in Him, our only desire that He may be glorified.

I often pray something like this: "Blessed Lord Jesus, possess me who comes before You now as intercessor. In union with yourself who lives to make intercession, I pray for N. I pray for the healing of his entire person; I pray that You will induce in him a trustful and serene mind." An attitude of trust and serenity tends to set free within those for whom we pray the power of the resurrected Christ.

We must beware always of the temptation to focus our attention on the brokenness for which we pray, rather than on Jesus who is even now touching those we bring before the throne of grace, healing and making whole each one. As in our mind's eye we see Him stretching forth His hand to heal, we see the sick, the bereaved, the suffering from any cause, transformed into radiant and joyous persons as the result of His life-giving touch.

Even as we pray, we remember His promises: "Anything you ask me in my name I will do" (Jn. 14:14); "Until now you have not asked for anything in my name. Ask and you shall receive, that your joy may be full" (Jn. 16:24). In the promises of Jesus, there is a qualifying condition: prayer must be offered in His name.

"If you live in me, and my words stay part of you, you may ask what you will, it will be done for you" (Jn. 15:7). This living, abiding, resting in Him and He in us implies a likeness to Christ, perhaps some understanding, however slight, of His eternal purpose of love.

As we pray for healing and total wholeness, we might well remember also that God is even more eager to heal than we are to be healed. The secret is to be able to receive Him who *is* our wholeness. It is not only that God is accessible and that we must approach Him. Even more, it is He who has already approached *us*, and we must be accessible.

Thank you, Lord Jesus, that today as always, you have been walking behind me to receive me when I fall. And now, you have clasped my outstretched hand, and raised me up. I pray now, blessed Lord, that you may raise and heal her for whom I pray.

Holy Mary, Queen of Heaven, you who know so well a mother's heart, intercede for my child.

Two Nights Later
(after healing service)

After the service tonight, someone said to me, "Of course you are claiming your daughter's healing." My answer was, "No. I am praising and thanking God that He is at work within her, but I do not believe in publicly claiming a healing when all the symptoms still persist." Why? Because I have seen too many hurt, too many disillusioned, and too much harm done the healing ministry as a whole, by premature public claims of healing.

Sharp in my memory is a recent mission when a gifted and zealous layman had been selected by the mission church to participate in the laying on of hands. During one of the informal sessions he announced that someone to whom he had ministered the night before had been healed. I rejoiced until he said, "I've told her that she must witness to this regardless of the symptoms." My heart sank. The reason for his conviction of healing? He had felt a sensation of heat in his hands when he had administered the healing rite.

In the first place, no promise of healing should ever be made to anyone. We are all too fallible instruments to dare to make such a claim. The mission incident just described exemplifies the danger of someone without knowledge (however great his gifts and zeal) working in the healing ministry. There are "sensible" manifestations of all sorts which of themselves in no way signify healing, or lack of it. These manifestations include sensations of heat or electricity, vibrations in the hands, and even being "slain in the Spirit." I am concerned for this woman if she is not healed.

Over the past few months I have gained a new appreciation of the Psalms. It is well past time for bed, but before retiring I glance over the Psalter. Suddenly, leaping off the page, I see the words: "TRUST IN HIM AND HE WILL ACT" (Ps. 37:5b). Thank you, Jesus, for this blessed and unequivocal assurance, with which I go to sleep tonight.

As I get into bed I seem to hear His voice, "Let not your heart be troubled. Have faith in God and faith in me" (Jn. 14:1). I have, my Lord and my God, and that You know. I commit her now to your never-failing love and care, knowing that You are doing better things for her than I can desire or pray for.

Tomorrow, the group on prayer; the day after, another mission. I am ready and fit to go, and I go with joy.

15.

Salvation, Healing, and the Love of God

July 22
Saint Mary Magdalene

"Almighty God, whose blessed Son restored Mary Magdalene to health of body and of mind, and called her to be a witness of his resurrection: Mercifully grant that by your grace we may be healed from all infirmities and know you in the power of his unending life."[1]

Mary Magdalene—healed by Jesus, His devoted follower, standing by the cross at Calvary. Mary Magdalene—heart-broken, weeping, beside the tomb. Not only have they crucified Him, but they have taken away her Lord and she does not know where they have laid Him. Mary Magdalene—her grief-stricken face suddenly flooded with rapturous wonder as she hears the beloved voice say, "Mary," and her ecstatic cry, "Rabbouni!" (meaning "Teacher"), as Jesus in His compassion reveals Himself to her. Mary Magdalene—the first witness to the risen Lord and the first messenger of the Resurrection, as she runs to the disciples, exclaiming in breathless excitement, "I have seen the Lord!" (Jn. 20:11–18)

A great many of us "saw" the Lord in a different but no less real sense during the mission a few weeks ago: one more demonstration of how those missions which would seem at the outset to be the least promising end up among the most blessed.

I had been apprehensive about this engagement for several months. (Lord, will I *never* learn?) As the missions are scheduled so far in advance, it is inevitable that occasionally the pastor who has made all the arrangements has left to go to another church before I arrive. Having learned that such was the case this time, I had followed my usual custom under such circumstances, of writing to the new clergyman, offering to withdraw. He answered by saying, "By no means. The people would not hear of it!" I took note of his reference to "the people," with no mention of any enthusiasm on *his* part.

As I met with the new rector in the sacristy the night the mission began, I saw that my apprehension had been justified. He appeared withdrawn and cold, and it seemed obvious that he indeed had *not* wanted the mission but had been overridden by members of the committee in charge of the affair.

At the usual mission there are at least five clergymen who participate with me in the laying on of hands. This time there were only two. It was clear that the pastor expected only a small turnout, in what he described as a "very conservative church and community." When we walked out to begin the service, we found every pew filled to capacity. With only three of us to administer the healing rite, the service lasted about four hours. I was gratified to observe that not one member of the congregation left until the end of this horrendously long service, and as a result it was blessed by an outpouring of the Holy Spirit of which all were aware.

The next morning, following the Eucharist, I spoke of the love of God and of how He does indeed manifest Himself to those who love Him (Jn. 14:21). I commented on the supernatural love of God, and of how, when we experience this love, we experience God, for love is not only *of* God (1 Jn. 4:7) but God *is* love (1 Jn. 4:16).

After I had spoken, the rector inferred, without directly saying so, that I was encouraging the "elitist" group in his church, those who felt themselves spiritually superior to the others, because, as he said, "Everyone does not experience God and His love in the same way." This is perfectly true, and sound criticism which I have taken to heart.

That night, the second of the mission, there were again only three of us to administer the healing rite. This time the pews were not only filled, but people were standing four or five deep in the rear of the church. The service lasted considerably longer than on the preceding night, and again and again I faced the altar praying for strength as the streams of people coming forward to receive the laying on of hands seemed endless.

At the conclusion of the service, I walked out with the clergy into the sacristy where the pastor offered a brief prayer. Then, leaving the priests to collapse from fatigue, I went back to greet the people. As I stood for a moment in the sanctuary and looked out over the church, a moving sight met my eyes: every aisle was filled with people kneeling on the marble floor. The presence of the Lord was almost palpable, and the entire church was in an awed and holy hush. No one wanted to move, let alone leave, nor did I, tired as I was. I knelt for a few moments before the altar offering God praise and thanksgiving and then began to thread my way through the still-kneeling crowd. Suddenly the silence was shattered by a voice from the back of the church, calling, "Mrs. Neal, come quickly. Someone has been hurt!"

Sending someone for the rector, I got back as quickly as I could to the narthex, where a knot of people were gathered. I looked out of the open church door. At the bottom of the outside steps lay a young man, prostrate in the snow, his crutches lying beside him. I ran down the steps to the unconscious form, calling over my shoulder to the group to pray with me. I knelt in the snow beside him and was aware as I prayed that a kind gentleman had taken off his coat and placed it around my shoulders as protection against the bitter cold and driving snow. The prayers of the people of God enveloped us all like a mighty wave. And then it happened, that which I have so often tried, and always unsuccessfully, to describe: the love of God pouring itself out upon us all in overwhelming abundance, that love which is at once Himself and His power to heal.

The young man stirred, opened his eyes, and sat up. Throwing his arms around me, he said, "Thanks." He was helped to his feet, unhurt as I knew he would be. He then walked off into the night, leaving his no longer needed crutches laying in the snow where they had fallen. As I walked back into the church, a chorus of voices spoke, "*Now* I know what you meant when you spoke this morning. I've never had an experience of the love of God like this."

On the last day of the mission I was asked to lay hands on two retarded youngsters. I prayed for their wholeness and, above all, that they might know the love of God. In answer, His love poured itself in and through and upon us. After the "Amen," I was greatly touched to see their radiant faces, and to hear them both say, haltingly, "Oh, Mrs. Neal, I love you so much." They were aware of, and had fully received, the abundant outpouring of God's love, manifested through each of us to the other.

Glancing at my watch I saw that it was almost time for the luncheon scheduled for clergy and physicians, so I retreated to the rector's study for a few minutes rest, having been on my feet all morning. Within seconds the rector came to find me to take me down to the luncheon. To my surprise, he threw his arms around me wordlessly, and led me to the parish hall. When he introduced me to the assemblage, he told them what the mission had meant to him, ending with, "My life will never again be the same." By this time I should be used to the miracle of God's love overtaking situations, but I seem never to get used to it!

That night, the final one, there were still only three of us to lay on hands. The church throughout the mission had been filled with clergy from Roman Catholics to Baptists, so I suggested that the pastor go out to the congregation before the service began, asking two or three to come up to help us. He dutifully tried, but as he saw no one he knew, he was understandably reluctant to embarrass a stranger who might be unfamiliar with the ministry of healing.

In the sacristy before the service started, all three of us prayed virtually the same prayer, "Lord, you know I've never been so tired in my whole life. Hold me up, please, and work through me however exhausted I am." God never fails to answer this prayer, for His strength is indeed made perfect in our weakness (2 Cor. 12:9). Then it is that we live and work in the power of Christ, knowing that we of ourselves *have* no power. And so it was on that last night.

As I said goodnight to those beautiful people, the love of God shining in their eyes, someone thrust something into my hand, with the words, "Wear this always, and pray for me, Athena." (Later I discovered that it was a rose ruby ring set in platinum.) Another lovely person put into my other hand a gift I shall always treasure, a blessed medal from the Chapel of the Miraculous Medal in Paris.

Finally getting back to the sacristy, I found the two priests, their arms around each other's shoulders, and their eyes tear filled. They opened their arms to me, and we stood embracing, enfolded in His love, as we praised God mightily for all we had experienced. The rector, transformed into a warm, outgoing human being, said that people in the church who had not spoken to one another since he had come were now hugging each other. That whole church was healed through the great ministry of reconciliation, and how beautifully and abundantly He manifested Himself to all of us, healing all brokenness of body, mind and spirit, as He brought hundreds of souls to Himself.

Lord, help us always to be obedient to the heavenly vision. Christ, enable us by your indwelling presence to shine as your light in a darkened world. Lord, be with us now and throughout eternity.

Yesterday a counselee came to me with a problem common to many Christians. She was suffering badly because her father whom she deeply loved was dying. He was elderly, and she was a good Christian, so it was not the fact that his death was imminent which primarily distressed her, but rather that he had not accepted Christ. "He's going to die without being saved," my counselee said in real anguish. "What can I do? Where have I failed in bringing him to Jesus? I've been telling my father for years that he must accept our Lord or he will forfeit his salvation."

While it is certainly our holy obligation as Christians to do what we can in and by the power of the Spirit to bring souls to Christ, I must believe on the basis of Scripture that we endure much unnecessary worry over the salvation of our loved ones. We might recall that Jesus did not convert everyone with whom He came in contact. We remember the parable of the Seed. The sower is sowing the word. Those sown on fertile ground listen to the word and take it to heart; those sown on fallow soil do not. Our Lord never lingered to try to batter people into faith (Mk. 4:15–20). He left it to them. "Come unto me," He says, but the "coming" must be voluntary, the free choice of each individual.

He commissioned His disciples to proceed in the same way. When He appointed the twelve, He told them that to whatever city they went, they were to proclaim the kingdom of God and heal the sick. However, Jesus cautioned the disciples (and to us who are also His disciples, the same caution applies), "When people will not receive you, leave that town and shake its dust from your feet" (Lk. 9:2, 5).

Therefore our commission as His followers is to preach the Gospel to all the world but with the knowledge that the entire world will not receive Him.

What, then, can we do about our beloved unconverted? First, pray as did Saint Monica for her son Augustine. She prayed for many years before her prayers were answered. It behooves us to do the same without discouragement. The one thing we should not do is try to *force* acceptance of Jesus on anyone.

"But my father is dying," my counselee expostulated. "There's no time for years of prayer."

I reminded her of the parable of the Laborers in the Vineyard (Mt. 20:1–17). Those who had worked only a very short time received the same wages as those who had labored all day under the scorching sun. When the owner of the vineyard was criticized by one of the latter for being unfair in his method of payment, he responded, "Are you envious because I am generous?"

To human minds and hearts, it may seem unjust that someone who has lived all his life as a pagan (and perhaps a scoundrel) can accept Christ with his dying breath and thus at the last second be "saved," while someone else may have lived his entire life committed to our Lord, appropriating the salvation He came to bring us all. Are *we* perhaps envious because of God's surpassing goodness and generosity?

No one knows what is in the heart of anyone else, and many an individual does not know himself. This is a knowledge fully possessed only by God.

To me, the parable of the laborers makes it crystal clear that God accepts deathbed conversions. "But what if my father dies in a coma?" asked my counselee. As the spirit never sleeps so is it never unconscious. Even as his Christian loved ones worry, the spirit of the unconverted is very probably even then, acknowledging Jesus as Lord and Savior.

My final advice yesterday to the suffering daughter was to stop worrying and start praying, and then leave the whole matter in God's all-merciful hands. All of us tend to underestimate the infinite mercy and love of God because it is so far above and beyond our finite understanding.

I think that because of our very zeal, we must all be on guard against self-righteousness. To torture ourselves over the lack of salvation of another may possibly be the sin of presumption on our parts. Just perhaps, the inference could be, "I am sure of my own salvation, but surely God can't accept so-and-so." Perhaps it is well for those of us who are committed Christians to concern ourselves with the salvation of our *own* souls, for we are clearly told that "the last shall be first, and the first shall be last" (Mt. 20:16).

In the final analysis we are utterly dependent on the mercy and love of God. It was because of His love that He came among us, and worked and suffered and died to bring us salvation. It is because of His mercy that He continues to save us today. I fervently hope and devoutly pray that we will be judged by His love and by our love for Him, manifested to others.

I remember how Jesus said of a woman nearly two thousand years ago, "Her many sins are forgiven . . . because of her great love" (Lk. 7:47). He might have said this also of Mary Magdalene.

Will You be able to say it of me, too, Lord? Only in your mercy and through your love.

16.

Joy Unspeakable

I got home from vacation the day after Labor Day. It was a wonderful holiday but I am glad to be home, despite the fact that after several weeks of trying to get back into the swing of work, I feel ready for another vacation!

Today is a major feast day, one which (as so many do) seems peculiarly applicable to the healing ministry. The archangel Michael plays an important part in apocryphal literature and is mentioned four times in Scripture: twice in the Old Testament (Dan. 10:18; 13:12) and twice in the New (Jude 9; Rev. 12:7-9). As a result of these scriptural and other apocryphal passages, the early Church recognized Michael as the protector of individuals against Satan, especially at the time of death, when he was believed to conduct souls to God. Not so widely known is the fact that he was venerated as a great healer, with many hot springs in Greece and Asia dedicated to him.

Until moving here, I had spent my entire Christian life in the diocese of Pittsburgh. My first bishop, the Right Reverend Austin Pardue, had a great interest in the subject of angels. I must confess I did not share it, seriously questioning their relevancy in this day and age. Then a few years ago, I led a mission in a Lutheran church, during which I met informally with an interdenominational group consisting of over one hundred men. The first question I was asked dealt with the subject of angels, and rather incredibly, we spent the entire two hours on this one question. I was astonished at the number of hard-headed businessmen who obviously derived great comfort from the thought of guardian angels with whom they could enjoy companionship and from whom they could expect protection. I decided then and there to take angels more seriously and to learn more about them.

I discovered that I had conveniently overlooked the many references to angels in Scripture. I had failed to note that they are, in a real sense, colorful threads woven into the fabric of the faith.

Primarily they are messengers of God, more than men but infinitely less than God. They most certainly are *not* those effeminate creatures with wings and flowing robes, busily playing harps, as depicted by medieval artists. They are, according to Jesus' teaching (Mt. 22:30), sexless, spiritual beings, intermediaries between man and God, who are privileged to enjoy the vision of Him in heaven (Mt. 18:10).

The New Testament writers represent Christ from His conception on, as surrounded by angels at the most important times of His life. Beginning with the angel announcing to Mary our Lord's conception and subsequent birth, angels ministered to Him in the desert as He underwent His temptations; they strengthened Him in His agony at Gethsemane. Angels met the women who went to the sepulchre, saying to them, "Why do you search for the living one among the dead? He is not here; he has been raised up" (Lk. 24:4–6); and we are told that angels will accompany Jesus at His Second Coming (Mt. 24:31).

I reread with new interest the accounts of the apostles led out of jail by an angel (Acts 5:19–21), particularly the extraordinarily vivid account of Peter. Scripture tells us that it was the voice of an angel who told Peter to get dressed and follow him. And as the apostle dressed, the chains he wore fell to the ground. The angel of the Lord then led him past the sleeping guards to the gate. It opened and Peter walked through. The angel followed him through one street, then left him. In re-reading this account, I noted that the angel was with Peter as long as his help was needed (Acts 12:7). This incident and others like it are not fairy tales; they are miracle stories.

How often one hears people say upon the death of a child,

"Now he (she) is an angel." However, according to Scripture, this child is not an angel, for angels are a separate category of beings created by God. They are like us in one respect: they have free will, and thus can choose between good and evil. According to the Book of Revelation, one of their hierarchy led a revolt against God. This was Satan who, with his horde of fallen angels, was cast out of heaven (Rev. 12:7–9).

Far from the sentimental picture we have of angels, they are described in Scripture as warriors. Michael did violent battle against Satan (portrayed as a dragon), which is why the Archangel is so often represented carrying a sword, either engaged in combat with, or standing over, a defeated dragon.

Saint Michael the Archangel; angels as messengers of God. In the Episcopal liturgy are the words: "Therefore we praise you, joining our voices with Angels and Archangels and with all the company of heaven" (BCP, p. 362). All of us sing about angels in such hymns as "Hark! the herald angels sing." I wonder if most people, like me, never really paid any attention to the words.

We are told that one of the tasks of angels is to assist us mortals as the angel of the Lord assisted Peter, and although we may disavow any belief in these heavenly beings, how often we say to someone who has helped us, "You're an angel to have done thus and so."

The Protestant tradition in general has veered away from the subject of angels, and there are reasons for this. However, only lately have I wondered why so many Christians of this day and age and of every branch of the Church seem to believe heartily in demons, while rejecting their angelic counterparts. I wonder why we are quicker to speak of Satan and his hordes of demons than to acknowledge the hosts of angels ready to do battle against them and to emerge victorious if we will just call upon them.

After a recent healing service, someone spoke to me of how frightened she was of becoming demon-possessed. I suggested she need not be frightened but just call upon her guardian angel appointed by God to protect her. She looked as blank as I would have not long ago. I think if we were all more aware of the protective power of the angelic host, there would be fewer cases of demon possession. The forces of evil are *not* stronger than the forces of good: demons are *not* stronger than angels, and certainly Satan is not more powerful than God.

Speaking purely personally, I believe in angels because I believe Scripture. I cannot deny the probability of spiritual aid from those beings whose mission is to serve God. Yet, having said all this, and although I continually need and seek all the spiritual aid I can get, I still have difficulty with the idea of anything or anyone who seems to come between me and my direct communion and communication with Jesus. Therefore I must admit that it is Jesus the Christ who answers my every need, who heals my brokenness, who alleviates all loneliness, who supplies my weakness with that strength which is Himself. And when I die, I somehow feel that *He* will take my hand in His, because according to His promise, where He is, there shall I be also (Jn. 14:3).

Despite this, I am able to pray with open mind and grateful heart the Church's Saint Michael's day prayer: "Everlasting God, you have ordained and constituted in a wonderful order the ministries of angels and mortals: Mercifully grant that, as your holy angels always serve and worship you in heaven, so by your appointment they may help and defend us here on earth" (BCP, 244).

October 4
Saint Francis of Assisi

This day has very special meaning for me as it is the one on which I customarily renew my annual vows as a Third Order Franciscan. The chaplain received my vows this morning at mass, and the blessing of Saint Francis, prayed over me, still rings in my ears: "The Lord bless thee and keep thee. May He show His face to thee and have mercy on thee. May He turn His countenance to thee and give thee peace. The Lord bless thee!" And so He has, beyond all my deserts.

I was life-professed as a tertiary years ago, as it seemed the closest I could come to the religious life to which I then felt called.

Within the Franciscan "family" founded by Saint Francis in the thirteenth century, there are three orders: the first, comprised of brothers (friars) and sisters; the second, the Poor Clares of Reparation and Adoration. These are religious, living in their respective houses under the traditional vows of poverty, chastity, and obedience. The Third Order, originally known as Brothers and Sisters of Penance, now simply as "tertiaries," is composed of laypeople and clergy, married and unmarried, living in the world in the spirit of the counsels and under rule. The three orders are bound together by their common aim to make Jesus Christ known and loved everywhere, the same aim as their founder had so many centuries ago. The outstanding characteristics of all Franciscans are those preeminently exemplified by the life of Francis himself: joy, humility, and love.

Saint Francis, the *poverello* (little poor man) of Assisi is one of the best loved of all the saints and probably one of the least emulated. Few of us in the world today share his fervent love of Lady Poverty. We who are tertiaries are bound only to live simply and without undue extravagance.

I have derived much satisfaction in living here in what, for me, is a very Franciscan manner. However, I must admit it is not as Franciscan now as it was when I first came. The community, considering that it fit into the category of "permanent improvement," has put in the most glorious bedroom closet for me, which runs the length of one whole wall. Curious how one's sense of values change: no longer do I take for granted a large closet. Having been without *any* closet in my bedroom for so long, I now feel I am living in the lap of luxury, and am unashamedly ecstatic!

Actually, I am afraid I am not a very good Franciscan as far as poverty goes. I have one seemingly uncontrollable extravagance: buying books. There is really no excuse for this, as the convent has a large and excellent library. The trouble is, that if I like a book I want to be free to mark and underline passages in it. Obviously this means I must own it.

I often think (but most especially when a newly ordered book arrives as one did today) of how, a long time ago, Father Paul told me that at the friary the brothers changed their cells (rooms) frequently. They could take with them to their new quarters only what they could carry in both hands. Anything more than this had to be disposed of. I look around a bit guiltily, as I realize that it would take a large van to move just my books! I rationalize this by calling my books the tools with which I work. In a sense this is true, but do I need so *many* tools?

Saint Francis, like the majority of the great saints, was both a contemplative and an activist, a combination of gifts I wish more of us possessed. We tend to be either-or people.

Francis spent his life preaching the Gospel, making known the Lord Jesus Christ and His love, spreading the spirit of brotherhood, serving others wherever there was a need. At the same time, he spent entire nights in contemplative prayer, the silence only occasionally broken by his cry, "My God and my all." He lived out the words of Saint Augustine, "Without God, I cannot; without me, God will not."

The key words of our lives as Christians today, as they were of Saint Francis, might well be, "I will give . . . ," and not only of our worldly goods, but perhaps even more importantly, of ourselves.

I often reflect on all the times I could have given more and wish that I had. And then, lest I embark on a guilt trip from which there is no return, I remember those times when I was dead-tired, and a call would come which meant getting out of bed, dressing and driving, perhaps many miles. (Everywhere I go seems to be twenty-five miles from where I am!) I recall faces bright with gratitude, and I offer thanksgiving to God that He got me out of bed and let me go in the strength of Christ. I pray that perhaps some good was accomplished in His name and for His sake. "I will give. . . ." This is a vital part of the Gospel message and as such, of the healing ministry.

With Saint Francis, I pray this day his prayer: "Lord make me an instrument of Thy peace; where there is hate that I may bring love; where there is offence that I may bring pardon; where there is discord that I may bring union; where there is error that I may bring truth; where there is doubt that I may bring faith; where there is despair that I may bring hope; where there is darkness that I may bring light; where there is sadness that I may bring joy. O

Master, make me not so much to be consoled as to console; not so much to be loved as to love; not so much to be understood as to understand. For it is in giving that one receives; it is in self-forgetfulness that one finds; it is in pardoning that one is pardoned; it is in dying that one finds eternal life."

Evening

Following the age-long custom of the Church, we had the blessing of animals in the chapel this afternoon. Frances, the all-American dog who belongs to one of the sisters but is in effect the "convent" dog, was first in line. Of course she has lived here a long time, and knows the ropes. In fact, she often comes to the summer services in the chapel, walking through the open door and lying quietly in the sanctuary, sometimes across the feet of the chaplain. On more than one occasion, I have had to step over her to get to the altar rail. As I love dogs, it delights my heart that the sisters do not even look up when Frances comes to mass; they take it for granted.

Next in line for her blessing was Jay-Jay, a beautiful dalmatian belonging to another of the sisters. Then came several cats followed by various and sundry other animals (including goldfish) brought by the village children. They all behaved with splendid decorum.

"Praised be my Lord by all His creatures." "Let every creature that is in heaven, on earth, and under the earth, and land and sea and all that is in them, Praise and exalt Him above all forever" (Saint Francis).

After Compline

"In my distress I called to the Lord and he answered me" (Ps. 120:1).

This has got to be the happiest day of my life! My daughter just called to report on a series of tests made a few days ago. The diagnosis of that dread disease is found to be erroneous. Her illness is due to an obscure ailment transmitted by insect bites this past summer. It is a self-limiting disease, and the doctor predicts no new "attacks." Praise God! Another case of "wrong diagnosis," which to the believing Christian means the power of God has been at work.

"Glorify the Lord with me, let us together exalt His Name" (Ps. 34:4).

I go on mission tomorrow with a grateful heart.

17.

Blueprint for Healing

October 23
James of Jerusalem

As I came home from mass today and put on the coffee, I began to think of the mission of two weeks ago, with a combination of thankfulness and amusement. Not more than perhaps a half a dozen times since I have been working in the healing ministry have I had the experience of too many people at a healing mission. This time the church was jam-packed. The doors were left open and people were standing in the streets as far as the eye could see, despite the fact that the parish hall with closed circuit television was filled to overflowing. As I walked into the church on the first night, it resembled nothing so much as the rush hour in a New York subway. On my way to the sacristy, I felt physically assaulted by the noise. Everyone seemed to be talking at the top of his or her lungs.

There is no denying the tremendous power of God manifested in a large crowd of praying people, people praising God simply because He is, not just because of His gifts. However, this night it seemed to me (perhaps because I like quiet and know God oftenest in the still, small voice) that the spirit of prayer was woefully lacking. For a few seconds my heart sank. However, I was relieved and thankful when the crowd calmed down during the brief worship service, and remained quiet and attentive during my long meditation. Then came time for the laying on of hands.

When the worshipers were invited to come to the altar rail, bedlam ensued. No one waited for instructions; the ushers might as well have not been there as people swarmed up from the undercroft, poured down from the balcony, and rushed in from the street. Hundreds clogged the aisles, all trying to come forward at the same time. Because they had to stand for so long before reaching the altar rail, the crowd understandably became increasingly restive and noisy, talking in loud tones, calling across the nave to friends on the other side of the church. I stopped the service at least three times in an effort to restore some order. Finally I was forced to say, "The Holy Spirit will absent Himself from here unless we are careful. He will not work in such chaos and confusion." At these words, those in the front of the church who could hear me, began to quiet down and the others gradually followed suit.

As is often the case at missions, the Episcopal bishop of the diocese was graciously participating in the opening service. I worried, "Oh, dear, I wonder if he thinks all missions are as rowdy as this. Whatever will he think?" I glanced at him out of the corner of one eye, and he seemed to be having a rather good time at this very untypical Episcopal service. Before the service, he had told me apologetically that he would have to leave early in order to catch a plane. After about two hours, he left for the airport. At the same time, the other participating clergy, except the rector of the church, departed. It took us nearly four hours to minister to the remaining congregation.

I ended by asking that a prayer vigil be kept during the next two days, between the end of the daytime session and the beginning of the evening service. This a number faithfully did. The following two nights there was a real spirit of prayer, and all of us being better prepared now to handle the situation, the remaining services went smoothly.

The Holy Spirit abundantly blessed the mission, and the healings were many, some spectacular. A man blind for thirty years opened his eyes and saw the altar, an autistic child spoke her first word, a woman bent with arthritis suddenly straightened. News of healings and blessings have been pouring in ever since I got home. I am very thankful to God.

When there are great crowds of people there seem to be more healings, simply because there are more people. The percentage of healings seem to remain fairly constant regardless of the number at any given service. Yet I have noted that usually, although certainly not always, there seems to be more actual power if there are a large number of believing Christians assembled together.

I recall that at Pentecost the Spirit was poured out upon a group "gathered together in one place," a group which was to be the Church. Through the coming of the Holy Spirit, the fellowship, the Church, was to be empowered. Does this mean, then, that our private prayers are useless? Of course not. Although the Spirit came upon a gathering, and thus His power was never to be a private affair, still *all* there were filled with the Holy Spirit (Acts 2:14).

To be sure, the expectant faith of a large group of believers seems actually palpable. Does this mean that He is more present in a large group than in a small? No. He offers Himself wholly to each individual. It is *we* not God who tend to react and respond to large assemblies of the faithful. It is we who are sensibly aware, who feel, emotionally, the faith of the others. This activates and increases our own, so that we each become more open to His love which is His power to heal, and to Himself in whom alone lies that abundant life He came to bring us.

I think of the words reportedly spoken at an opening healing service by a missioner from abroad. "Where are all your sick? I've never seen such healthy looking people!"

Obviously, the most serious and crippling sickness and brokenness can seldom be seen with the naked eye. For example, one cannot "see," a broken relationship, or the anguish of the recently bereaved. One cannot "see" that internal cancer which is silently destroying a body, or that damaged heart which threatens life. But I knew what that missioner meant. He saw no wheelchairs, no one on a stretcher.

I reflect that the phenomenon of apparently increased power at large gatherings is manifested also in those services where the visibly sick are brought. Again, it is *we* who are reacting. The response of God is *always* there for anyone who will receive what He is so anxious to give: Himself. Perhaps when we see with our physical eyes the lame, the halt, and the blind, we are subconsciously reminded of the earthly ministry of Jesus, when the sick were brought out to the streets on their pallets, and He walked among them, blessing and healing. Perhaps it is because when we see with our physical eyes those who are in need, we are lifted out of our own self-concerns and our hearts go out in the love of Christ, while our prayers speed to the throne of grace. There is a great unity and centering of prayer on others. We feel that prayer power, and curiously enough, when we so focus our hearts and prayers on others, we frequently find ourselves healed of brokenness, whatever it may be.

I glance over the mail on my desk some of which I must answer tomorrow. I chuckle at the letterhead on one of the envelopes. Inside is a beautiful note from the bishop who had participated in the last mission. Far from being offended by what seemed to me the bedlam of that opening service, he tells me that that night was one of the high points in his spiritual experience.

The bishop's response, as contrasted to my own, is just another demonstration of the subjectivity of human reaction, as opposed to the objectivity of God's presence. His presence is not conjured up by our imagination or emotional response, but is always there, always indwelling each of us; and His healing power is not summoned up but *released* by faith, and available to each of us according to our ability to receive and His most holy will.

My train of thought this morning is not to be wondered at, as today we celebrate the feast of Saint James of Jerusalem, who is presumed to be the writer of the Epistle of James. It is on the last chapter of this epistle that the healing ministry of the Church is patterned.

"If anyone among you is suffering hardship, he must pray" (Jas. 5:13). The word "hardship" is variously translated as "suffering" (KJ), "afflicted" (RSV), "in trouble" (Jerusalem and Phillips). Regardless of the precise translation, the meaning is clear: such hardship or affliction is differentiated from physical sickness. The wide scope of the healing ministry is thus unmistakably defined: it embraces all brokenness in every area of our lives. The verse immediately following gives specific instruction for the physically ill.

"Is there anyone sick among you? He should ask for the presbyters of the church. They in turn are to pray over him, anointing him with oil in the name of the Lord." This prayer, uttered in faith, will reclaim the one who is ill, and the Lord will restore him to health. If he has committed any sins, forgiveness will be his. Hence, declare your sins to one another, and pray for one another, that you may find healing. The fervent petition of a holy man is powerful indeed" (Jas 5:14–16).

The sick, then, are to call for the prayers of the faithful (those who know with their minds and believe in their hearts that Jesus does indeed heal today as He did two thousand years ago). They are to ask for the sacramental healing rite of anointing with oil (holy unction), to be administered by those in the Church authorized to do so.

For long years unction was not used publicly for healing because of its association with the Last Rites of the Roman Catholic Church, which association with death was as firmly entrenched in Protestant as in Roman Catholic minds. However, the Second Vatican Council restored unction to its original purpose, as a rite which emphasized physical healing. This change in format and intention was made, as Pope Paul VI declared, "in view of the words of James." As a result, anointing with oil has come back into its own as the specific sacrament of healing the way it was used in the ancient Church.

A growing number of Roman Catholic churches (and not only those with a charismatic emphasis) now hold healing services on a regular basis, using both the laying on of hands and unction.

We lay on hands because Jesus did, among other methods He used to heal. We anoint, first because Jesus authorized this means of healing (Mk. 6:13), and, secondly, because the Epistle of James urges us to use this rite. Thus both rites are equally valid and both are used in today's healing services, either interchangeably or together. Unction, among the five sacramental rites evolved in the Church under the guidance of the Holy Spirit, is, for me, a "special" means of grace. For this reason I prefer to use it less frequently than the laying on of hands. Although anointing all those in hospitals who desire it, our custom at Saint Thomas Church is to use unction only once a month, unless there is a particular need or request for it more often.

Later

Thinking of unction has reminded me that last night I received an interesting telephone call telling of an instant healing.

The story actually had its beginning the night I returned from the mission. It was very late when I was awakened by the ringing of the phone. On the line was a priest whom I had met once during a mission in his area. In a voice so weak as to be nearly inaudible, he told me that he was alone on a camping trip in Northern Canada, many miles from civilization and thus from either priest or physician. At that moment he was hemorrhaging badly from a bleeding ulcer. Would I pray for him over the telephone? Before I could answer, he said, "Wait! I feel as if I'm going into shock. I have blessed oil with me as always. I feel as if I *must* have unction. Can I anoint myself?"

I had not the remotest idea how to answer him. And then I heard myself say, "Get the oil and bring it back to the phone with you." In an instant he was back, and I said, "As I begin the sacramental formulary, I'll be spiritually anointing you. But you dip your thumb in the oil and anoint yourself as I pray, making the sign of the cross on your forehead."

I proceeded with the prayer: "I anoint you with oil in the Name of the Father, and of the Son, and of the Holy Spirit. As you are outwardly anointed with this holy oil, so may our heavenly Father grant you the inward anointing of the Holy Spirit. Of his great mercy, may he forgive you your sins, release you from suffering, and restore you to wholeness and strength. May he deliver you from all evil, preserve you in all goodness, and bring you to everlasting life; through Jesus Christ our Lord" (BCP, p. 456). We joined together in a firm Amen and hung up.

Last night the same priest, now safely home, called me. Hemorrhaging had stopped simultaneously with the words, "Restore you to wholeness and strength." Upon his return home, he had told his physician what had happened. The latter immediately ordered the appropriate tests, the results of which the priest had just learned and had called to tell me. The ulcer of some years' standing was now completely healed. The only thing wrong with him was a slight anemia, "apparently due to loss of blood in the recent past."

As I prepared to go to mass this morning, I pondered what had transpired. Did it mean we should go about freely anointing ourselves? No, that would be contrary to the instructions of Jesus and would violate the sacramental principle which is closely tied in with the functioning of the body of Christ as a body and not just one individual. To me, the lesson to be learned from this healing is that in the mercy of God, He honors our spiritual intention. I was with that priest with my entire spirit, and with my spirit, empowered by the Holy Spirit, he was anointed. Perhaps, I reflect, this episode could be likened to the making of a spiritual communion. This was Holy Unction by spiritual intent. Once again we have a demonstration of the goodness of God, who honored our use of one of the means of grace He has given His Church and prevented one of His priests from "bleeding out."

I think of the prophecy of Isaiah and rejoice that it has been fulfilled: "He will come and save you," we are told. "Then the eyes of the blind shall be opened, and the ears of the deaf unstopped" (Is. 35:5).

He *has* come; we *are* saved; and at the touch of His healing hand, the lame do indeed leap as harts, and the tongues of the dumb do indeed sing.

The Epistle of James makes very clear the close correlation between the forgiveness of sin and physical healing. Time and time again I have seen this demonstrated. And were I asked to state one of the primary requisites for healing, I would surely answer: confess your sins with a contrite heart and then *accept* God's forgiveness. It is His absolving grace which alone can cleanse our hearts so that the Holy Spirit in all His power can flood the open channels of our beings.

It is perfectly true that God will never permit Himself to be confined to any one invariable method (not even James's), to any one set of rules and regulations, to any one prayer which guarantees the healing we seek. Nevertheless in my experience, I have noted the healing virtue in His absolution.

I have frequently observed a simultaneous act of contrition and physical healing, or a healing immediately followed by such an act. I have also seen healings occur in those who, by their own admission, have flouted every spiritual law we know anything about. Nevertheless, in the vast majority of cases, I have seen a definite correlation between healing and forgiveness. I believe that without repentance in the healing picture, there cannot be wholeness.

"My son, your sins are forgiven. . . . Stand up! Pick up your mat and go home!" (Mk. 2:5, 10)

I have done a great deal of speaking in local churches this month, and there could hardly be a more apt time to speak on the healing ministry. Saint James' feast today, and only five days ago, on October 18, we celebrated Saint Luke's day.

I am speaking again tonight, and there will be a healing service. There is no doubt what the Scripture reading will be. However, I think I'll add the Saint Luke's day prayer, which I greatly love and daily make my own: "Almighty God, who inspired your servant Luke the physician to set forth in the Gospel the love and healing power of your Son: Graciously continue in your Church this love and power to heal, to the praise and the glory of your Name; through Jesus Christ our Lord" (BCP, p. 244).

18.

The Problem of Guilt

October 28
Saints Simon and Jude, Apostles

Fall is my favorite time of year, and my heart sings as I walk to mass in the crisp, clear air, the brilliant colors of the foliage celebrating, as am I. Celebrating what? Life!

However, unaccountably, my mind was not where it should have been during the Eucharist today. For some reason my thoughts kept reverting to the woman, overcome with guilt, whom I counselled yesterday. I find myself, hours later, still thinking of her and of the whole subject of guilt.

There are certainly times when our feelings of guilt may be legitimate. However, I know all too well the number of people who suffer real anguish because of imagined guilt. They often require skilled psychotherapy as well as spiritual counsel. But just now, on this lovely autumn day, I am concerned with neither of these categories, but rather am I pondering the prevalence of basically emotionally healthy Christians who are guilt ridden. I am concerned because we, of all people, presumably know the Source of all forgiveness. Is it that we do not believe, in our hearts, that He pardons? Or could it be, I wonder, if the now outmoded teaching of the Church has burned itself into our unconscious, that teaching which stressed the judgment of God to the exclusion of His mercy? Whatever the cause, I grieve because our failure to accept His unstinting forgiveness must break the heart of God, somehow negating the sacrifice of our Lord who came to reconcile us to Himself, offering us the inestimable gift of continuing forgiveness if only we will offer Him our contrite hearts.

It is something of a paradox that through the healing ministry we can be healed of our affliction of guilt, while at the same time this ministry seems to offer its own particular reasons, albeit totally invalid, for feelings of culpability. If, for example, we are seeking the healing power of God for ourselves and do not receive it precisely when and how we think we should, we tend to blame ourselves, our personal lack of faith, forgetting that the ancient Church never placed the entire onus for faith on the individual concerned, but rather on the body, the Church.

Or we may feel that our healing is delayed because of our sins, which may or may not be true. But in either case, the remedy is the same: to examine yourself without morbidity, ask the forgiveness of God, and then *accept* it. Having done this, confidently leave the rest to Him. I think, with gratitude to God, of those who have awaited their healing perhaps for years, never ceasing to pray expectantly, and of the spiritual giants they have become during their waiting period. I think of the many who, when finally healed, have said to me, "Just suppose I had given up! But God kept me going on in faith."

The woman who came to me yesterday (and who started this whole train of thought) was guilt ridden not because she, herself, had failed to receive healing, but because her husband had not. She blamed the weakness of her faith and therefore the inadequacy of her prayers for him.

The healing ministry is fraught with paradoxes which can only be resolved by the Holy Spirit. For example, we know that complete wholeness can never be attained on this earth, but only through death; yet we are bound, as Christians, to do all we can through God, to safeguard the gift of life He has given us.

"He [one] must ask in faith, never doubting" (James 1:6). In my experience these words have engendered more guilt than faith. And so it was with my counselee yesterday. "My faith wavers, and I know it," she said in despair, "but I can't *help* it!"

A very wise priest once offered me advice which I have never forgotten, and I passed it on now.

"If there ever appears to be conflict in Scripture," he said, "look only to Jesus for your example, and listen only to Him and to no one else, not even St. Paul."

Thus I reminded my counselee of the anguished father two thousands years ago who, seeking the healing of his son, said to Jesus, "I do believe! Help my lack of trust" (Mk. 9:24).

Our Lord honored this prayer as He honors ours today. One of the many wonders of the Incarnation is that He lived among us, truly man as well as truly God. Thus he *understands* the difficulty of an unwavering faith, and honors even our *desire* to pray with full expectancy, just as He honors our desire for holiness, our desire to be rid of sin.

Guilt fostered by what we feel is the inadequacy of our prayers is, first, to fail to recognize that *all* prayer is in some respect inadequate; and second, there seems to be in many of us an unconscious conviction that by praying "correctly" we can manipulate God into doing our bidding. The truth is, of course, that God will not be manipulated by prayer, sacrament, our attitude, or anything else. He is sovereign.

I ponder anew the complete sovereignty of God, and re-read the magnificent statement of His sovereignty found in Job. "Where were you when I founded the earth? ... Have you ever in your lifetime commanded the morning and shown the dawn its place? ... Have you entered into the sources of the sea, or walked about in the depths of the abyss? Tell me, if you know all: which is the way to the dwelling place of light, and where is the abode of darkness? Have you fitted a curb to the Pleiades, or loosened the bonds of Orion? ... Do you know the ordinances of the heavens; can you put into effect their plan on the earth?" (Job 38). I love these words and all the words in this chapter of Job. For reasons I do not fully understand, it is a great comfort to me to know that God cannot be manipulated and is utterly sovereign. And yet His very sovereignty leads to tensions within the healing ministry.

I believe without equivocation that wholeness is God's perfect will for us, yet I am fully cognizant of the truth that "My thoughts are not your thoughts, nor your ways my ways, says the Lord. As high as the heavens are above the earth, so high are my ways above your ways and my thoughts about your thoughts" (Is. 55:8-9).

If His ways are not our ways, how then can I believe unequivocably that wholeness is God's perfect will for us? Because of the teaching and example of Jesus in the Gospels and reflected throughout the New Testament. Because we see the results of obedience to His command to heal the sick in the early postapostolic Church and in today's healing Church. Because the very nature of God is perfection and not brokenness of any kind.

As a Christian I believe that ultimately His will must be fulfilled in all things. Any seeming paradoxes in Scripture are resolved not by our own intellect but by the Holy Spirit who, Himself, being the Spirit of Truth, reveals to us all truth (Jn. 16:13): a truth not in conflict with, but higher than, any attainable intellectual knowledge. In a very real sense, we who are Christians must deal simultaneously with the "now" and with all eternity.

Someone said to me the other day, "I'm not willing to 'go out on a limb' for the healing ministry." I could only counter with a question: "Dare we, then, 'go out on a limb' for the Gospel itself? Are we promising those to whom we take it, a salvation which does not exist? Are we offering them a pie-in-the-sky religion based on fantasy and founded on wishful thinking?" If we dare not "go out on a limb" for the healing Christ, then surely we dare not present the Gospel which in every way is a healing Gospel, while the Savior who heals today as surely as He healed two thousand years ago is one of the clearest revelations in all of Scripture.

In thinking of guilt today, I consider the need to be sensitive to all with whom we come in contact, but most especially within the context of the healing ministry where so many being peculiarly vulnerable can be badly, however inadvertently, harmed.

I recall all too clearly a mission of several months ago, and feel the same sense of outrage that I experienced at the time. I saw in two very badly damaged individuals, once again, the devastation, physical, emotional and spiritual, which can be wrought by guilt. In the case of this man and this woman, it was a guilt unfortunately and inexcusably engendered during a healing ministry two years prior to my visit.

The man had been told at the earlier mission that his illness was punishment for his sin, a cruel, untrue, and unscriptural assertion (Jn. 9:2). It had caused two years of needless suffering. Obviously he had over-reacted, manifesting the extreme vulnerability of the sick. He knew with his mind that God would forgive no matter what the sin, but it frequently happens that the heart's

cognition of God's forgiveness depends upon a human interme-
diary.

I could not give him absolution, but I could and did give assurance of pardon. I prayed that his heart might be opened in the
name of Jesus and by the power of the Spirit, that he might be enabled to receive the forgiveness of God. That day he was healed of
his guilt, and his shining face was an inspiration to me throughout
the rest of the mission. At the final healing service, he was healed
of his physical disability, which, incidentally, had caused him far
less pain than the guilt.

As to the woman, wife of a Protestant minister, she came to me
during the mission, pouring out her story of guilt and misery. She
had had both breasts removed some years before, had told the pre-
vious missioner of her surgery, and asked for prayer that the fear
of recurrent cancer might be taken from her. Instead of so praying,
she was told that the breast cancer had been caused by a poor relationship with her mother and the many resentments she
nourished. Until her relationship with her mother improved (particularly traumatic, as her mother, with whom she had a very good
relationship, had recently died) and until she got rid of the resentments in other areas of her life, the cancer, she was told, most certainly would recur. This story seemed to me so unbelievable that I
asked her husband to confirm it; he did.

I talked for a long time with this tormented woman, and have
rarely seen anyone so free of resentment. (*I* was the resentful one
at this point—over her treatment!) For two years she had driven
herself to the brink of breakdown, trying to find what wasn't there.
Again, an over-reaction, and for the same reason, and also an example of how the self-probing process can be overdone, degen-
erating into scrupulosity (spiritual nit-picking). This is why I advise people to spend no more than three or four minutes in daily
self-examination, lest they become morbidly introspective, precisely what had happened to this poor woman.

She had suffered the physical and psychological damage of having a double mastectomy, and now was bearing the heaviest of all
her burdens: that of guilt. The trouble was, she didn't know what
she was guilty *of.*

The Lord healed her of guilt and of her fear of cancer. However, what needless suffering had been caused by an almost brutal insensitivity!

Blessed Lord, I know that I cannot be the only person working in Your ministry who never inadvertently hurts people. Grant me, Jesus, just a tiny share of your boundless love and sensitivity, and forgive me for any hurt I have ever inflicted. There is so much suffering in this world, let me not add to it by giving pain to any one of Your children. As we know, Lord, that it is in You and through Your blood that we have been redeemed and our sins forgiven, so it is through Your blood that we are healed. May we remember always the immeasurable scope of Your power in us who believe (Eph. 1:7, 19), and may You guide us as we attempt to use this power for Your glory.

It is beginning to be apparent that I shall *never* be able to find my way in the Book of Hours the community uses for its offices, at least on feast days like today's. Bless the sisters who come to my rescue by leaving a little note on my prayer desk listing the various pages. Very occasionally one of them makes a mistake, and this helps restore my ego at least for that day!

I had particular difficulty today on the feast of Saints Simon and Jude, perhaps because I was thinking alternately of my counselee and what a beautiful day it was and thus had trouble concentrating. However, I had my wits sufficiently about me to listen to (and to *hear*) the prayer for this day, certainly a fitting way to end this month: "We pray that, as they [Simon and Jude] were faithful and zealous in their mission, so we may with ardent devotion make known the love and mercy of our Lord and Savior Jesus Christ" (BCP, p. 194).

In the Gospel for this day (Jn. 15:17–27), Jesus tells His disciples that not only the Holy Spirit will bear witness to Him and to His works, but His disciples must also bear witness. As we, too, are His disciples, Jesus is speaking to us and to all generations of

Christians. It is our sacred duty as well as privilege to witness to our Lord, who is indeed the same yesterday, today, and forever (Heb. 13:8). If He still has the power to forgive sins, and we know that He has, so also has He the power to heal, and thanks be to God we know that He does.

I love the beautiful doxology of Jude, and often use it in missions: "Now to him who is able to keep you from falling and to present you without blemish before the presence of his glory with rejoicing, to the only God, our Savior through Jesus Christ our Lord, be glory, majesty, dominion, and authority, before all time and now and for ever. Amen" (Jude 24–25 RSV).

19.

Our Beloved Alive

November 2
All Souls' Day

Yesterday was All Saints' Day, that day (although not the precise date) set apart since before the fourth century to celebrate all Christian saints, known and unknown. This morning, at the altar, our beloved dead (or as I think of them, our beloved *alive*) were mentioned by name. However, on this particular All Souls' Day, my heart and mind are filled with but one thing: Sister Virginia. She who never complains has been complaining of severe pains in her back and legs.

At mass today, she looked extremely well. I chided myself for worrying about her, and reminded myself that one of the worst aspects of cancer was fear of recurrence. Had I fallen into this trap? I believed that she was healed. Why now was I wavering? And yet I found myself wondering if on next All Souls' Day, her name would be on the list of the faithful departed now being read. Suddenly my heart seemed to stop: I was certain that I had just heard the name of Sister Virginia Cecelia mentioned. But that was utterly ridiculous. She was sitting in the oratory.

This uncanny experience has remained with me all day. What did it mean? Was it a premonition, or simply a trick of the imagination? The answer was given in the weeks ahead. She was to die, at the age of fifty-eight, a beautiful and holy death. As I watched her die, I thought of how she once said to me, "I read somewhere that frequently, if they pray hard enough, people are granted the boon of dying as they might wish." I am far from sure if this is true, but I know it was so in the case of Sister Virginia.

She had gone into the hospital for tests. On the day I went to visit her, she was just finishing lunch. To my question, "Any news yet from the tests?" she shook her head. At that moment her physician walked in. One look at his face, and I knew why he had come and that the news was bad. As he began to speak, I reached for her hand. The tests had revealed cancer throughout her body. She received the verdict without flinching, but as soon as the doctor left, she said with great anxiety, "All I'm worried about is my father. He's an old man, and this news will kill him." (An aged man to be sure, but one of amazing strength; it did not.) I stayed at the hospital with her for three hours. Neither one of us abandoned hope of her healing here and now, but we faced the possibility that this might not occur.

Just before leaving Sister Virginia that day, I prayed for her and anointed her, and together we thanked God that in His goodness I had been with her when she received the devastating news.

It was four o'clock when I started home in a state of semishock and exhausted by the emotion-draining three hours I had just spent. Caught in the rush hour traffic, it seemed forever before I reached the convent. At last I turned in at the gates, breathing a sigh of relief, only to be met by the acting chaplain who rushed out to tell me that close friends of mine from Pittsburgh had just called to say they would be coming to the convent to spend the night and would be arriving within the hour. My heart sank. I had no intention of burdening them with my distress, and I wondered how I could maintain a facade of good cheer throughout the evening.

I went in, threw myself on the bed, and prayed that my guests would be late. Within minutes there was a knock at the door. There they stood, aglow at our reunion and in anticipation of our going out for a festive dinner together. I asked for fifteen minutes to change my clothes, most of which I spent praying that the Holy Spirit would enable me to "carry off" the evening. As always, He came to my rescue.

Sister Virginia was to be transfused a number of times, but after each transfusion her period of well-being seemed shorter. Two weeks before her death, she went into the hospital for the last time to receive blood. This time she returned not to her own room, but to the infirmary. I was glad of this, for no one is permitted in the Sisters' private wing, but I could visit her in the infirmary.

In her last nine days, she never missed a full day's work as bursar of the community, nor did she miss a single mass or office with the exception of Compline. She retired early, asking me to visit her each evening after she was in bed. We began most of these evenings by reading Compline together, after which we talked for about an hour. Over these nine days, I watched with something akin to awe, the climax of her lifelong striving for holiness and that perfection to which we are all called as Christians.

She complained of no pain, only that her very keen mind was not as alert as it should be. Each passing day her frustration increased because, as she put it, "What I used to do in ten minutes seems to be taking me longer and longer."

I observed her carefully each day at mass, as gradually her face took on the unmistakable hue of the terminal cancer patient. At the same time, there was a curious luminosity about her. Though we sat on opposite sides of the oratory, it seemed to me that even with my eyes closed, a brightness shone from her which pierced my eyelids.

On what was to be her last day here, although I did not know it then, she came to mass as usual but appeared obviously weaker than the day before. I was saddened to think that she would have to miss the Saturday night Prayer and Praise meeting which, to her joy, had recently been inaugurated. Clearly, she would not be well enough tonight to go anywhere, except to bed.

I had been fasting a great deal during the days just passed, and as I had lost considerable weight, decided that I had better eat that night, whether or not I felt like it. To tempt my nonexistent appetite I went to the market and bought two thick lamb chops, a luxury I normally forgo because of the price. I had just put them in the broiler when the telephone rang. It was Sister Virginia. "We're waiting for you," she said. "You're late, Emily. Aren't you coming to the Prayer and Praise meeting?"

I gulped, said "Of course," turned off the broiler, and flew. On the way I kept thinking how wonderfully good of God to enable her to go to her beloved meeting.

The large room was filled. Sister Virginia, almost too weak to sit up, was trying to play the guitar. She looked up and smiled as I came in, and another sister took over the guitar from her. I was grateful and infinitely thankful that so many of the sisters who ordinarily were not interested in this type of meeting were there tonight. I knew why.

We sang and prayed, and then Sister Virginia said, "My healing is going to be very rapid from now on. Praise the Lord!" Her face seemed to illumine the whole room.

When the meeting was over, two sisters, one on each side, took her, literally carried her, back to her room. I was walking directly behind them, and she turned back to me and said, "Emily, please come visit me tonight after I'm in bed. Give me about fifteen minutes." Foolishly, I remonstrated, "You're too tired. Let's skip tonight." Thank God she was insistent, so I sat in the foyer of the convent for fifteen minutes and then went back to the infirmary.

She was safely in bed, and rejoicing over the meeting. "You know, Emily, that's the first time sisters so-and-so ever went. Isn't it great that they were there?" she said delightedly.

Then began what was to be our last talk. For the rest of my life I shall treasure that visit. I cannot reveal what was said, but I shall always be thankful to God that when it was necessary for me to respond, He put words in my mouth. At the end, Jesus, Himself, stood there. "Put your hands in His, Virginia. He will lead you in that unknown way, and it shall be safer for you than any known way." She and I embraced, our tears commingling, and she said, "I can sleep now." I replied, "Yes, you are forever safe in the everlasting arms." And so she was, and is.

As I went out the door she said, "Emily, I'm *so* glad you're here." Those were the last words I was to hear her speak.

On my way out of the convent, I met Sister Ann who was sleeping in the infirmary at that time in order to meet any need which might arise. I hastily scribbled my unlisted telephone number on a scrap of paper and handed it to her. "Please, Sister Ann, put this on your bed table. The convent has my number, but I have no idea where they keep it." She embraced me, smiled, and nodded.

At about three o'clock in the morning, my phone rang. It was Sister Ann. "Mother Louise and two of us are here at the hospital. Sister Virginia is in a coma." I both asked and stated, "She is dying." "Yes," came the reply. "I'll come at once," I said, and hurriedly dressed. I grabbed my Prayer Book, marked the section "Ministration at the Time of Death," checked my holy oil stock, and was off.

Someone on the hospital staff had been alerted and was there to meet me as I drove up to the emergency entrance. She took me straight back to where Sister Virginia lay. I anointed her first, this time as the Last Rite, the ultimate healing, then prayed the beautiful prayer of commendation at the time of death: "Depart, O Christian soul, out of this world; In the name of God the Father Almighty who created you; In the name of Jesus Christ who redeemed you; In the name of the Holy Spirit who sanctifies you. May your rest be this day in peace, and your dwelling place in the Paradise of God" (BCP, p. 464).

Just then the acting chaplain arrived. Taking the Host from the pyx, he touched it to her lips: "The Body and Blood of our Lord Jesus Christ, keep you in everlasting life."

He led those of us gathered around the bed, in the Creed, the Our Father and the Angelic Salutation. Then we lapsed into the silence of our private prayers, the stillness broken only by the sound of Sister Virginia's quiet breathing. Gradually the pauses between breaths lengthened, until she took one deep breath, and that was her last. At that moment, she stepped out of the shadows into the light.

It was almost time for Sunday mass when I got home. The community knew: the chapel bell had tolled just minutes after her death. (Lawrence, the head of the maintenance team, was to say to me next day, "When the tolling of the bell woke me, I prayed so hard it wouldn't be for Sister Virginia, but in my heart I knew it was.")

I was grateful to the Mother Superior and the sisters for calling me to the hospital so that I could be with her at the end, which is also the beginning. And God's hand in the matter was most apparent as Sister Ann told me later what had happened.

Sister Virginia had tried to get out of bed in her infirmary room and had fallen. In the adjacent room Sister Ann heard her fall and ran in. Sister Virginia was conscious for only a few moments. Her last spoken word was the name of Jesus.

The nurse unable to bring her to, Mother and the two sisters had taken her to the hospital. When Sister Ann went to call me, she realized she did not have my unlisted number. And then suddenly she remembered the scrap of paper which I had asked her to place on her bed table. She reached into her pocket, and there it was. That she, who habitually forgets nothing, had forgotten to leave it in her room was surely one of God's "coincidences."

When I was asked to preach the homily at Sister Virginia's requiem mass, I was honored, but my first reaction was, "No. I could never get through it." Then I thought for a few minutes and changed my mind, for I realized this would be the last gift I could give my beloved sister. So I agreed, with deep gratitude for the privilege.

The chapel was filled to overflowing, a tribute to Sister Virginia and a sign of the countless lives she had touched. As the chaplain preceded the casket, those glorious words rang out, "I am the resurrection and the life, saith the Lord; he that believeth on me, though he were dead, yet shall he live; and whosoever liveth and believeth in me shall never die" (Jn. 11:25–26).

No one ever believed more ardently than you, Sister Virginia, so of *course* you live, and far more fully than we who are here today. Thanks be to God that you have passed from death to life (1 Jn. 3:14). "I know that my Redeemer liveth . . . and though this body be destroyed, yet shall I see God . . . and not as a stranger" (Job 19:25–26).

Yes, Virginia, you see Him and no longer as in a glass, darkly. You know now, even as you are known (1 Cor. 13:12).

"At the hour of my death call me, and bid me come to Thee, that with all Thy saints, I may praise Thee forever and ever" (*Anima Christi*).

So at last, Virginia, you are wholly with Him. You have joined the great chorus, and I hear your voice singing above the rest, as I so often heard it in the convent choir: "Alleluia! Salvation, glory and might belong to our God" (Rev. 19:2).

I sat in the choir with the sisters. Those that passed me, touched my shoulder. I felt their love and prayers as I hope they did mine.

I spoke that day in the power of the Spirit and never was I more thankful.

Thanks be to God for the life of Sister Virginia, for what she meant to so many, and to me.

Thanks be to God that she is now completely healed and totally whole in Him.

Thanks be to God that we do not grieve as those without hope, for we know Him who *is* our hope (1 Thess. 4:13).

Death and resurrection: broken hearts and joy unspeakable. We weep, but only for ourselves. Joy for her transcends our sorrow.

Thanks be to God for the blithe and joyous spirit of Sister Virginia which will always pervade the community she loved so much.

Above all else, thanks be to God who has indeed given us the victory through our Lord, Jesus Christ (1 Cor. 15:57).

Of course, at mass this morning, Sister Virginia's death was yet to come, but as it eventuated, I had received that which was more than a premonition: it was a glimpse into the future. And in my heart, I knew now what was to come. A long time ago when I wrote of my husband's death,[1] I remarked that in the years which lay ahead for me, I believed I would remember most clearly not the grief but the joy of knowing my Lord so close. This has proved to be true, as it will be true of Sister Virginia's death.

Thank you, most holy Father, Creator of all that is, that purely by grace I know You, however imperfectly, the one true God.

Thank you, Lord Jesus, my Savior and Redeemer, that You live and that I know it. Because You live, there is no death, and "they that love beyond the world cannot be separated by it" (De Koven).

Thank you, Holy Spirit, Sanctifier of the faithful, for your enabling power, your consolation.

Thank you, Holy, Immortal, One, the Triune God, for the knowledge of my heart which surpasses in wonder all other knowledge.

20.

Be Expectant

I love to celebrate whatever the occasion, and seize upon the slightest excuse for festivity! Therefore it pleases me greatly to celebrate three new years: the secular one on January 1, the day my work year starts in September, and above all the Church's new year which began yesterday on the First Sunday of Advent.

I think this season of joyful expectancy is my favorite of the church year. From now until December 25 we await the coming of the Lord Jesus, He who has already come yet is still to come. We await Him, who though He comes every second of the day—indeed continually indwells us—yet is born anew in our hearts in a different and special way each Christmas Day.

These four weeks before Christmas used to be known as the "Little Lent." In general, this is no longer true, but the keynotes of the season are still and always will be the same: penitence, expectancy, and joy. (These could also be termed the keynotes of the healing ministry.)

The other night some of us were discussing the meaning of Advent. Someone commented, "This is a season of anticipation and unmitigated joy. Penitence has no place in it."

However, for me, penitence and joy are two sides of the same coin. This is not some personal idiosyncrasy, but the teaching of John the Baptist as I understand it. "Reform your life! [repent]," he cries. "The reign of God [joy] is at hand" (Mt. 3:2).

Penitence, like sin, is an unpopular word; even our churches avoid it as much as possible. Yet penitence during Advent is a far cry from sackcloth and ashes, rather is it the oil of gladness (Heb. 1:9).

A contrite heart is not one bowed down by guilt; it is a heart *delivered* from guilt, for it is offered with the knowledge of immediate forgiveness. And therein lies the essence of our joy, not that we have no sin but that we are forgiven. "O Saviour, merciful and tender. . . . Joy beyond all excess of joy, that Thou dost take away the burden of my sin!"[1]

Advent is a glorious season indeed, but also a solemn one. Solemn because we seek, insofar as possible, and by God's grace, to become a fit habitation for the King of Kings. I think back, now so many years ago, when my husband and I brought home each of our new babies from the hospital, how sparkling clean we made sure the nursery was, how pretty and immaculate the waiting crib. How much more, then, should I seek to have the cradle of my heart pure and beautiful to receive the Holy Child.

Last week a woman, looking downcast and dejected, came to me for counselling. As she told her story it was evident that she had reason to be unhappy, but happiness and joy are by no means synonymous. The unhappiness caused by personal circumstances has nothing to do with that joy of the Lord in which lies our strength. However obscured it may sometimes seem to be as we feel ourselves overwhelmed by difficulties, there remains at the core of our beings, that joy which no one and no adversity can take from us.

I began by feeling sorry for my counselee, but halfway through her recital it became clear that she did not need my sympathy. She felt so sorry for herself that anyone else's sympathy would have been superfluous. There passed through my mind the episode of Peter tempting Jesus to self-pity and of how quickly the Lord rebuked him for this (Mt. 16:23).

It was near the end of our session, when the woman sitting opposite me said, "As you can see, none of this is my fault. As a matter of fact I don't believe I have *ever* committed any sins."

I was slightly aghast at this statement, and she must have seen my expression, for she quickly said, "I've never done anything really bad, like stealing." Then, hesitantly, she asked, "What *is* sin, anyway?"

I tried to explain to her that sin was any rebellion against God, any flouting of what we know to be His will. Few of us are robbers or murderers, but *all* of us give to Him less than we can of our hearts, ourselves. Our surrender of self to Him is *always* less than complete; our prayer life can *always* be improved; our devotion always increased.

"This is my commandment: love one another as I have loved you" (Jn. 15:12). How many of us do this without reservation, without qualification? I reminded her of how Paul has said that we *all* have sinned and come short of the glory of God (Rom. 3:23).

It was certainly not my prerogative to "rebuke" this poor woman nor yet accuse her of sin. I merely tried to point out to her that self-pity, in itself, is cause for penitence.

Before she left I prayed that by the power of the Spirit her heart would be opened to know her need for forgiveness, for all her sins known and unknown; that by grace she might be enabled to accept that which we all need and which He stands so ready to give, His absolution. It was she, not I, who added, "Lord, forgive my self-pity."

As she walked out the door, the gloom which had enshrouded her had largely dissipated, and she looked almost happy. The problems for which she had come to me would take many more counselling sessions to resolve. However, the greatest of these, of which she had been unaware, was already solved: her need for forgiveness had been met. She had already begun to learn that a penitent heart is a prelude to joy.

I wonder as I sit here now, how I could possibly be truly joyful that God exists and that I know it, how I could be honestly thankful that the Father has sent His only begotten Son, and that Jesus has sacrificed Himself for me, unless there were an element of sorrow for what I know to be my own unworthiness? Without this knowledge on the one hand, how can I possibly know joy on the other?

You gave yourself for me, Lord. What have I done for You? The answer must be, "So pitifully little." Unless I am aware of this, how can I know the fullness of joy? Lord, forgive, and by your grace uniquely proffered to a contrite heart, enable me to give more. The only way I can *give* more is to receive more of you, my Lord, more of your life that You may visibly live in me, more of your peace that I may pass it on to others in need, more of your joy that I may be for You who are the Light of the world, a reflection of that Light.

This whole season is one of exciting expectancy as we await His rebirth in our heart, as we await His healing touch upon our spirits and our bodies.

"Come, O Lord, and do not tarry." *Expecting* that He will come, that He will make us whole in the way that matters most, we pray with full anticipation that our God may come. He never disappoints us.

Joy is the beginning and the end of Advent. As penitence is simply the other side of the coin of rejoicing without end, so Christian expectancy is not vain hope, but sure and certain knowledge. It is this knowledge possessed by the Christian which gives us joy unspeakable: the knowledge that God loves and cares, that He redeems and saves, that He makes us every whit whole in Himself.

I think of the wonder of the Incarnation, and today it seems to me that one of its greatest joys is my knowledge that "He has been there." I know that wherever I go, I find Him waiting for me, strengthening, upholding, empowering by His Spirit.

I hear continually in my heart His words: "I will never desert you, nor will I forsake you" (Heb 13:5). And He never has.

"I am with you always, until the end of the world!" (Mt. 28:20). And He is.

I just picked up my mail at the convent. The first letter I read was from someone asking about the possibility of counselling with me on a regular basis. She needs help, she says, in learning to know herself.

This letter causes me to reflect that next to "Love and do what you will" the maxim "Know thyself" must be the most abused. I suppose it is because we who are alive today, regardless of age, are members of a lost generation, or is it a lost era? Paradoxically, the fact that we are an "I/me/myself" society seems largely responsible for our personal lostness. Then, too, we are living in a psychologically and psychiatrically oriented age which can contribute to what often appears to be an obsession for self-discovery.

No one has a higher regard for these two indispensable disciplines than do I, and no one is quicker to refer those who require more specialized help than I am equipped to render, than myself. My concern is that so many seek it who do not need it, and in such cases prolonged psychotherapy weakens as does the use of any crutch, making cripples of those who unnecessarily use them. Again, ironically, the very concentration on self which psychotherapy must demand if it is to be effective frequently tends to defeat its own purpose. The effort to "know thyself" can degenerate into a neurotic introversion which may make it impossible to discover one's true self. This danger is of course averted if pastoral counselling goes hand in hand with psychotherapy so that the whole person is ministered to.

I well understand the need to "know thyself" and I, myself, went through a considerable struggle before I finally learned that I could not hope to find myself, except in Him, for Jesus transcends and is larger than my own ego. In short, I was to learn that the "secret of my identity is hidden in the love and mercy of God."[2]

After thus reflecting, I must now check my counselling schedule and answer that letter. I pray that the writer will come to know as have I (but hopefully faster!) that "If I find Him, I will find myself, and if I find my true self, I will find Him"[3]

"Prepare the way of the Lord. Make straight a highway for our God!" (Is. 40:3).

This is the call, the underlying theme, of Advent. Last week I suggested to "my" people at Saint Thomas that this season is a good time to improve upon, or strengthen, or conscientiously try to live by, our rule of life. We need such a rule of prayer more than ever now, in the holiday season, to serve as a solid foundation beneath our feet so that we may the more firmly follow the glory that goes before us, and at the same time, to ready our hearts for Him who is yet to come. It will greatly help to prepare the way if we increase, by only five minutes each, our prayer time, our reading of Scripture, our spiritual reading.

I know well what a busy time of year this is, but I also recall the response of Martin Luther when someone remarked to him, "You are so terribly busy just now, I wonder how you have time to pray at all."

"Simply because I *am* so busy," he responded, "I have had to double my prayer time."

Penitence, expectancy, joy—and the greatest of these is joy, that characteristic which pagans in the early days of the faith noted above all else in those people called Christians: a people who lived joyfully, who withstood persecution joyfully, who went to their deaths joyfully.

During this season in particular, we who are His followers should know and, let us hope, manifest this same joy. We live in a darkened world, but each of us who believes is a candle which helps dispel that darkness, a candle lit by Him who is the Light of the world.

As Christians, we celebrate life; we run towards it, not away from it. We pray with Saint Teresa, "Lord, if you would prove me by trials, then give me strength and let them come!" So we hold out our arms and embrace life, never rejecting it, not even its pain, for we are awaiting once again the miracle of the Incarnation, the Word made flesh who humbled Himself to be born in a stable, who for all time was, and is, a revelation of God's compassion, as He comes to us in temptation, in poverty, in suffering. In His sacred humanity He has endured it all.

During the four weeks ahead we come nearer and nearer to the meaning of Christmas, that wondrous time when once again a completely new Life, a new quality of life for us all, comes into the world. And that Life makes it possible for us to have a different and living relationship and communion with Him, which forever changes (as it has already changed) our lives.

And now, O Lord, You who were conceived by the Holy Spirit, born of the Virgin Mary, and became man, I pray you to make my heart a fit habitation for yourself.

After Compline

It is unbelievable! I have been fighting off a cold all week but now it has apparently developed into a full-fledged case of bronchitis. I, who am never sick, am somewhat embarrassed—bronchitis twice within a few months! The sisters, bless them, try to cheer me up by telling me it takes time to become adjusted to the climate here. How long?!

Nevertheless, I go on mission tomorrow morning. Ordinarily missions are not scheduled between Thanksgiving and Christmas, one practical reason being that people are too busy to take three days out. However, rather than wait for two years, the church where I am bound decided to risk it. Between the time of year and my cough, things do not look too auspicious at this moment.

"Almighty God, give *me* grace to cast away the works of darkness, and put on the armor of light" (BCP, p. 211).

And now to bed.

21.

The Doctors' Mission

L ate last night I returned from mission, and what a mission it was!

At most missions there are a few physicians in attendance, but at this one there were so many, and so many became involved, that I shall always think of it as the "doctors' mission."

With a tendency to believe that by this time every church in Christendom must be aware of the healing ministry, I am rather frequently brought up short. This mission was one of those times. Having arrived the day before the mission was to begin, I had a long talk with the rector of the church. He told me that not only did the people in his locality know virtually nothing of the ministry of healing, but they were strongly prejudiced against it. It seems their sole contact with the ministry had been via television evangelists whose methods they cordially disliked. The reason the pastor had been anxious for my mission, he said, was that people might learn the difference between revivalist ministries (of which some are excellent, incidentally) and the sacramental ministry of the Church. The problem was to get people to come and see. By the time our talk was over, I was ready to go home before the mission began, convinced (almost!) by him that the church would be empty for the entire three days.

I did a lot of praying that afternoon, and was delighted that night to find the church well-filled, though far from overflowing.

Once again I was to see the truth reaffirmed: God will not be boxed in. I frequently tell people that *expectant* faith is a necessary ingredient for healing, and for those who acknowledge the healing

Christ I believe this to be generally true. However, at this particular mission I am reasonably certain that *no one* expected *anything*
to happen. Yet things never *stopped* happening.

Probably the first miracle was a personal one. Having a terrible
cough when I left home, I never coughed once throughout the
mission! I could only think, "Will I *never* learn to trust the Lord?"

At the end of the first service, people spoke to me rather diffi-
dently. A few said in very low tones, as if afraid they might be
overheard, "I think maybe I was healed tonight." One woman,
however, had the courage of her conviction, and said loudly,
"Praise God! I was totally deaf and now I can hear." As she went
out the door she flung over her shoulder, "My husband is an ear
specialist. I can't wait to tell him what happened!" (He came the
following night to see what was "going on in that church.")

After everyone had left, I turned to walk back to the sacristy
when someone called my name. As I turned back, a well-dressed,
attractive man in his mid-forties came up to me and said urgently,
"Could you have supper with me tonight? I understand you don't
dine before the service." I hesitated a moment and he said, "Please.
It's important." I looked at the pastor of the church, standing a few
feet away. He nodded, "It's all right. He's a member of the
church."

We finally found a restaurant open, and my host told me his
story. He was a physician and, as such, he had no intention of attending the mission. However, as a member of the vestry, he had
been "conned" (his word) into going by his rector, in order to set
a "good example for the rest of the church."

He had a very bad back, he told me, so bad that he was contem-
plating giving up his practice. When it came time for the laying on
of hands, he rebelled. "I never promised to submit to *that*," he said
with a smile. He stood up to let others go past him, and then
quickly decided to take this opportunity to escape! As the others
went up to the altar rail, he planned to sneak out the front door of
the church. But everyone in the church was moving forward, and
he found he could not "navigate against the traffic." Thus, unable
to walk in the opposite direction, he was swept along with the
others. He said, "I had to stand until I thought I would die, and
then at last I found myself at the altar rail." As everyone else was

kneeling, and he did not want to appear conspicuous, he painfully got to his knees, finding himself so hemmed in that he was forced to kneel upright with his hands at his side instead of on the rail which would have steadied him. "With even more strain on my back," he continued, "I figured right then that this healing mission would put me in the hospital." Finally it was his turn to receive the laying on of hands, and with a sigh of relief, he carefully arose to his feet, and was halfway back to his pew before he realized that his back was not hurting. "For the first time in four years," he told me jubilantly, "I am without pain," whereupon he leapt to his feet in the restaurant and touched his toes with the palms of his hands.

He attended every session of the mission thereafter and made a wonderful witness as a formerly unbelieving doctor.

Next morning, when the question and answer period was about to conclude, a gentleman stood to ask the final question. He prefaced his query with the statement that he had inoperable cancer, with three to six months' life expectancy; that he believed in God, but knew virtually nothing of the healing ministry. In answering his question, I addressed him as "Doctor." "How did you know I was a doctor?" he asked. I haven't the remotest idea, but for some reason I have an almost uncanny knowledge when it is a physician speaking.

He explained, and I know how true this is, that as a physician who understands so well the physiological processes involved, he found it difficult to believe that he could be healed. "But," he went on, "also as a physician, I've seen so many medically inexplicable healings occur that I know that there *are* miracles."

As our time that morning was limited, he asked if I would meet with him after lunch. This was easily arranged, as we were staying at the same motel. In our conference I learned that the doctor was not yet fifty years old, and that he believed there was still work for him to do. Because of this and his wife, he wanted very much to live. We had a long talk, and he opened the way for me to speak of death. I was glad of this, for it gave me an opportunity to emphasize that in death was the only complete wholeness for any of us. Nevertheless, I reminded him that as Christians we are called to have released, by grace, all the spiritual power we know anything about in order to preserve life. I also reminded him of the Nobel

Prize winner, Dr. Alexis Carrell, who, like him had found miracles difficult to believe. But Dr. Carrell, at Lourdes, saw the power of prayer at work when a cancer disappeared before his eyes.

Before I left, I anointed the physician, and the small motel room in which we were became a shrine, hallowed by the presence of God. We were both drenched in His love which poured itself out upon us.

As the doctor and I started to leave the room, he called me back. "I want you to know," he said, "that *now* I believe that I can be healed in the name of Jesus." He paused for a moment. "But you know something? If I had my 'druthers,' and if it weren't for my wife, I'd opt for dying to this life, so I could live in a new and glorious way fully with Him." Saint Paul's words flickered across my mind: "For, to me, 'life' means Christ; hence dying is so much gain" (Phil. 1:21).

I shall not forget this beautiful Christian, and do hope someone will let me know the outcome for him.

That night at the healing service, I had hardly opened my mouth to speak when the P.A. system broke down. It was a large church, and I had to speak at the top of my lungs for forty-five minutes. By the end of the service I was virtually voiceless. The last two people to leave the church were a man and woman who asked if they could speak to me. (As long as *they* were to do the talking, that was fine with me!)

The couple was, it seems, a physician and his patient. The woman had, with great difficulty, persuaded her doctor to attend the service. It was he who told me of the instantaneous disappearance of a tumor on his patient's neck. He was flabbergasted. This time *I* played the devil's advocate, and asked him if the disappearance of the tumor could not have been coincidence. He responded with a loud "No." (Several weeks later, I received an unsolicited letter attesting to this healing.)

When I returned to my motel room that night, I was touched to find several warm and gracious notes, all from physicians who had been at the service. Aware of my gradually disappearing voice, they all offered help, asking me to call them at their offices next day if they could be of service. One of these notes was from the physician-husband of the woman healed of deafness. Fortunately during the night my voice was restored, and the loudspeaker was repaired in time for the morning service.

The final day was the clergy and doctor luncheon. For the first time in my experience, there were many more physicians there than clergy. At the time for questions, one of the doctors raised his hand and said, "I would like to know how to bring my patients to believe in the healing Christ." At this a chorus joined in, "I want to know the same thing." Then one of the physicians made a remark which amused me. "Where are the clergy in this? Like all of my fellow doctors, I'm terribly busy. It's all I can do to handle my practice. I just wish the clergy would do their share, and not leave the 'converting' to us." Very true, but let it be said that in most places the clergy do do their share!

So many healings there were I cannot recount them, but I shall long remember a little boy who came up to the altar rail, obviously alone. He said to me as he knelt, "Ma'am, is it all right to bother God about pigeontoes?" When I replied, "Of course," he said, "Then I want to pray that He will straighten my feet." After the laying on of hands, I watched the little boy as he walked back to his pew, his feet now perfect. The Lord who said, "Let little children come to me," had touched this child with His healing hand.

I remember, too, the lovely young couple who were Baptists and had recently opened a religious bookstore. It was not doing well, and they had come to all the services to pray that, as it was His work, He would prosper it. A message for me before I left for the airport told me that that very morning they had sold three hundred dollars worth of books. Furthermore," the note said, "several ministers from the mission stopped in and said that from now on they would order all their books from us. Praise the Lord!" Praise the Lord, indeed!

Coming home on the plane yesterday, my mind was still on the mission. There was one woman who had made herself literally sick by worry, both over what she felt were wrong decisions made in the past and great anxiety over the future. She said, "If it is true that God never permits a greater burden than we can carry, then why do so many of us crack up and have nervous breakdowns?" Having myself been the world's champion worrier before I became a Christian, I could identify with her problem and assure her that God does indeed keep His promise: that He will *not* let us be tested beyond our strength. Along with every test, He invariably gives us a way out (1 Cor. 10:13). The reason many people do crack up is that they carry a triple burden, of past, present and future. This is contrary to the teaching of Jesus who tells us to live one day at a time (Mt. 6:34). The "way out" for all of us, is to "cast all your cares on him because he cares for you" (1 Pet. 5:7). The tragedy is that we are so busy fretting over a past that is finished and a future yet to come that we have no present at all. To learn the "way out" is to go to Him again and again, laying burdens of worry and anxiety at the foot of the cross. The time will come when we finally hear with our spirits His words: "Let not your heart be troubled, neither let it be afraid"; "As the Father has loved me, so have I loved you; abide in my love" (Jn. 14:27; 15:9). By His love we are healed.

As the plane stewardess came by with coffee, I was recalling the woman whose twenty-year-old daughter had recently died of a brain tumor. On the first day of the mission, I talked with her mother privately, and my heart broke for her. There are no human words to heal so grievous a wound, and the answers to such tragedies no one of us on earth can have. The only answer and all the comfort must come from the Holy Spirit Himself. I prayed that He would put some words in my mouth this day which might bring a modicum of comfort. "Spirit of the living God, pour out upon this mother the fullness of your grace and consolation."

I found myself speaking of the foreknowledge of God, though this in no way means that our lives are predestined. In terms which are inadequate but perhaps can help us understand, it is as if God stood on a mountain looking down upon a river. From this vantage point He is able to see the whole river at one time, as it were. He can see the river spread out before Him, which we might call the present. On one side, looking toward the river's source, He can see behind the bends, which we might call the past. On the other side, looking toward the sea, He can see above and beyond the curves, which we might call the future. In this crude analogy we can catch, perhaps, a glimpse of understanding as to what the simultaneity of time means in the eyes of God; how He knows and sees, at one and the same time, past, present, and future. This is the timelessness of God, which does not mean that everything that happens to us is foreordained. If it were, the gift of free will given us by Him would be a travesty; it would make no difference *what* we did if our futures were predestined. We know that it *does* make a difference, that our growth in holiness and wholeness is of supreme importance. And all along the way, we have the God-given privilege of free choice. He has a plan for each and every one of us. To this plan we can say Yes or No. What God sees in our futures is the end result of our having exercised free will.

As I talked, I pointed out that perhaps it might be that the failure to heal her young daughter was the ultimate mercy of God: that "severe mercy" of which C. S. Lewis writes in one of his letters.[1] In the timelessness of God, He may well have foreseen intolerable pain for this twenty-year-old girl.

I could speak from personal experience when I remarked that when we truly love we want to spare our loved ones all hurt. Even as I spoke I remembered so clearly how it was after my husband died. I knew great joy for him, but I, myself, suffered the usual anguish of the bereaved. And yet throughout that time, I recalled thanking God a thousand times a day that it was *I* who was suffering, and not my husband.

This grief-stricken women and I prayed together at the close of our session, and I was moved that she ended by thanking God for keeping her daughter safe. She attended all the healing services, and she was blessed by the Lord of all mercy, as He gently lifted her from the morass of her insupportable grief. Sadness remained, of course, but the hopeless despair was gone.

As the plane began its descent into Cincinnati, I was still thinking of miracles. I realized once again and with a new cogency, that a miracle is not primarily an act of overwhelming power on the part of God. Rather is it the kingdom of God made manifest in a unique way, under certain conditions, at certain times, and in certain places. The mission just completed had been such a miracle.

Just before the plane landed, I made Pascal's prayer my own: "I ask from Thee neither health nor sickness, neither life nor death, but that Thou mayest dispose of my health and of my sickness, my life and my death, for Thy glory, for my salvation and for the service of Thy church and of Thy saints. Amen."

People are too busy this time of year to write letters. So thanks be to God, when I returned home I found not the usual mountain of mail to be answered, but only a little hill. Now I am almost all caught up, and can enjoy the rest of Advent where I belong.

And so to bed: "Thank you dear Jesus, for all you have given me; for all you have taken away from me; for all you have left me" (Saint Thomas More).

22.

"My Lord and My God!"

December 21
Saint Thomas the Apostle

After mass today I re-read with joy a letter received yesterday from a priest in whose church I had recently led a mission. He comments on the strong sense of Christ's presence during those three days; of how denominationalism was swallowed up by the consciousness that we were all, from Roman Catholics to Pentecostals, simply members of the body of Christ assembled in the presence of our risen Lord and Head. "I felt," he wrote, "as if we had slipped back in time and were with the early apostolic Church, sharing its faith and practice. Perhaps, indeed, in a mystery, we were." And then he remarked on the extraordinary love he had experienced for strangers and friends alike, throughout the mission.

Love is the strongest force on earth. All theologians agree that God does not coerce us, and this is true. Yet He loves and by His love draws us inexorably and irresistibly to Himself. It is Love Incarnate whose rebirth we await now.

I think of Paul's words, "He who loves his neighbor has fulfilled the law" (Rom. 13:8), and I remember the man who came to me several months ago for counselling. He had begun by saying, "Well, at least I'm keeping the first and great commandment. I certainly love God with all my heart and soul" (Mt. 22:37). Before I could respond, this good man had launched into a diatribe against his next-door neighbor.

The difficulty is, of course, that the first commandment cannot be separated from the second: to "love your neighbor as yourself." I reflect how it is often much easier to love God whom we have *not* seen, than to love the neighbor of whom we may have seen too much! The way is not easy and He never said it was. "If you love those who love you, what credit is that to you?" Jesus asks. "Even sinners love those who love them" (Lk. 6:32).

Jesus prays for those who crucify Him; the apostles pray for those who martyr them; the Pope prays for his would-be assassin; a couple prays for the killer of their son. All Christians are called to pray for those who persecute them.

I think of the Russian starets who accepted the precept "Love your enemies" as the infallible criterion of Christian living. He used to say, "If you would know the extent of your fall, measure yourself against these words, 'Love your enemies.'" For most of us who so measure ourselves, the fall, alas, is apt to be very great indeed.

What can we do, when despite our efforts we are unable to rid ourselves of resentments and thus to really love someone who may have hurt us, or more importantly, someone close to us such as our children or our spouse?

There are a number of people (including myself) for whom two methods have worked wonders. The first I have mentioned in chapter 4, namely, holding up the one *you* cannot love, in the love of God. I have never known this method to fail if persisted in for a sufficient length of time. Whether, during this prayer process, we ever come to *like* such an individual is not of primary importance. Few of us like equally all those with whom we come in contact. Even Jesus had a "beloved" disciple (Jn. 20:2). However, by grace, we can love *all* in Christ, to the extent that we are ready to offer even our lives if necessary for those whom we may not like.

The second method sometimes can accomplish even the miracle of *liking:* do something nice for the one against whom you harbor resentment. This proves as effective as Saint Paul indicates! (Rom. 12:20)

I was reminded of this today when I read a letter from the counselee mentioned earlier. He writes that the neighbor whom he thoroughly disliked (and for good *human* reason) suffered a heart attack while mowing his lawn. His family being away, it was my counselee who called the ambulance and rode to the hospital with the stricken man. "Never in my life have I prayed more fervently than for my neighbor on that trip to the hospital." As he prayed, he experienced, in a wonderful way, the love of God which, he said, "filled the ambulance." My friend obviously responded by actually *loving* his neighbor back to life. The neighbor made a good recovery, and my friend says, "I really love that man now. I think he's the closest friend I have."

Jesus says, "This is how all will know you for my disciples: your love for one another" (Jn. 13:35).

Every drop of love in one's heart adds to the pool of love in the world, both today and in all the ages to come. It will never be expunged. We cannot love except through God, and this is as true of unbelievers as it is of the faithful. As God exists whether or not we acknowledge Him, so is He the God of the atheist as well as of the believer.

This afternoon on the way to do some last minute Christmas shopping, I passed a beautiful nativity scene. I parked the car for a few minutes so I could enjoy it, and realized anew that it is due to Saint Francis that millions of us over the years have enjoyed and been inspired by such Christmas scenes. The nativity scene, the crèche, was his gift to the whole Church.

It originated in a small town in Italy called Greccio. Francis' purpose was to depict in the most graphic way possible, the humility of the Incarnation. The saint's highest intention, always, was to observe the Gospel in all things; to follow the teaching and walk in the footsteps of Jesus. The humility of the Incarnation, that God should have come to the world as a helpless infant, greatly moved Francis. Three years before his death he conceived and turned into reality that which had been a long-held idea.

In the little town of Greccio, there lived a man by the name of Giovanni whom Francis deeply loved. The saint called for him two weeks before Christmas and said, "If you would like us to celebrate the feast of our Lord here at Greccio, please go at once and carefully prepare what I tell you, for I wish to do something very special which will vividly recall the memory of the little Child who was born in Bethlehem. I want to set before our physical eyes, in some way, the circumstances of His birth: how He lay in a manger; how with an ox and an ass standing by, He lay upon the hay."

When Giovanni heard this, he did as Saint Francis told him: he ran and prepared in the place designated by Francis the scene of Jesus' birth.

Finally came the day of great rejoicing, the holy day of the nativity. The Franciscan friars were called from wherever they happened to be at the time. They found the manger prepared, the hay brought in, and now the friars brought in the ox and the ass. At that moment, Greccio became a new Bethlehem.

The mass was celebrated over the manger, and it is said that the priest had a unique and wonderful experience of God that day. Saint Francis was vested as a deacon (in his humility he refused ever to be priested), and with his beautiful voice he sang the Gospel. At its conclusion, he preached to the people gathered around the crèche. He spoke of the birth of Jesus, and of His rebirth that day in all their hearts. He spoke at length of the nativity of the King who was to be servant of all. He referred to Jesus as the Child of Bethlehem, and we are told that as he spoke, his face was aglow with the holy radiance and love of Christ.

God's gifts were manifested in a marvelous way. Among other things, a vision was seen by one of the men clustered around the crèche. In it he saw a tiny Child lying in the manger, but the Child he saw was lifeless. Then, in the vision, he saw Francis go to the Infant and arouse Him, as if from a very deep sleep. This vision had deep meaning for the people on that day so long ago, and it has the same meaning for us today. The meaning is clear: Jesus had been forgotten in the hearts of many, but by the power of the Holy Spirit, He was brought back to life through His servant, Francis.

Finally, the solemn night celebration was brought to a close, and each person there returned to his home, filled with holy joy. Some time later, the place on which the manger had stood was made sacred, and an altar was built and finally a church erected there. Where once the animals had eaten hay, there the Blessed Sacrament of our Lord's body and blood was received for many generations to come.[1]

I thought of all this as I gazed at the nativity scene on a busy highway in a large American city. I was again thankful to Saint Francis for having given us so much, and to God, for having given us Francis.

Later

We think so often of the power and majesty of God, but today I think of the holy Infant. Though He was rich, yet He became poor, Saint Paul says (2 Cor. 8:9). And here indeed was poverty. The King of heaven takes His place among us, lying in a manger where oxen feed on hay. But there is no squalor here: it is a poverty made holy and glorious by Him, a poverty through which we have been made inestimably rich.

He came, and He comes again each year, in great humility, the only begotten Son of God. We know that Jesus lives for we are "eye-witnesses of his sovereign majesty" (2 Pet. 1:17). At the same time, as He is born anew, we are "eye-witnesses" of the gentleness of God. He came, and He continues to come, in that "divine gentleness made visible in a child in a manger."[2]

God is so many things to me: Creator of the world, Father, Abba, Friend, Master, Lord of my life, always. But today I feel with Saint Bernard, above all else, "Little is the Lord and exceedingly to be loved."

"To his own he came, yet his own did not accept him" (Jn. 1:11). His own still do not accept Him. This is why some will not believe in the healing ministry. This is why a man said of a certain church, "I won't go there anymore. All the minister ever talks about is the love of God and Jesus." This is why some say to me (with commendable honesty), "I won't go to the altar rail to receive the laying on of hands because I know I will be healed, and I'm not willing to commit my life to Christ." This is why some, though celebrating Christmas, refuse to acknowledge the dim but unmistakable outline of a cross which can be seen far beyond the crèche.

However now, the feast of the nativity nearly here, all of us know only the joy. Like the shepherds of long ago, we see the star gleaming brightly in the heavens, and in anticipation our hearts sing, "Glory to God in the highest, and peace to His people on earth."

"I am the way, and the truth, and the life," He says (Jn. 14:6); and that Life which is all Truth and the Way for all Christians has come into the world. I ponder the gifts of the Spirit: prophecy, healing, tongues, and all the rest, and know that they are as nothing compared to the greatest gift the world has ever known: that of the Son of God, Himself, given us not only that we may have life everlasting, but that glimpsing the kingdom here and now, we may know on earth something of the abundant life He came to bring.

Today I find myself wondering if, in our eagerness to bring souls to Him, we may think too much of "coming to Christ" and not enough of His coming to us. It is when He comes to us and we fling wide our hearts that we receive Him who is our life, our strength, our health, our wholeness, and our holiness. "Here I stand, knocking at the door," Jesus says. "If anyone hears me calling and will open the door, I will enter his house and have supper with him, and he with me" (Rev. 3:20). I ponder these words and remember, "Any who did accept him he empowered to become the children of God" (Jn. 1:12). In this power we have our being and our life; by this power we can do all things through Christ who strengthens us; through this power we overcome all things which are not of the kingdom.

But I am getting ahead of myself. It is in the straw of poverty that a small Child will lie again. It is before *Him* that we kneel in worship and adoration, before Him whose life among us began in a crib in a manger at Bethlehem, that life which was and is to change the world.

"God is born and the powers tremble—The Lord of the heavens lies naked. The star fades and the brilliance turns to shadow—the Infinite accepts limitation. Despised—reclothed in glory, the mortal—the King of eternity."[3] This is the mystery of the Incarnation.

As we celebrate the feast of Saint Thomas the Apostle, I began the day, as I always seem to on December 21, by feeling confused. Earthbound as I am, it seems curious to celebrate a post-Resurrection event (which is the one most of us associate with Thomas) before our Lord is yet born! However, in a very real sense, there is deep meaning in this as I invariably come to realize. Thomas, the doubter, the pragmatist, who would not believe until he had probed with his own fingers the nail prints in Christ's hands, and thrust them into His side. He listens to the words, "Do not be faithless, but believing," and Thomas responds with his magnificent confession of faith, "My Lord and my God!" (Jn. 20:27–28 RSV), the first explicit confession of His divinity. So the words of Thomas are indeed applicable as we prepare ourselves for Christmas, and kneeling before the Holy Infant, cry with Thomas, "My Lord and my God!"

After Compline

Tomorrow I leave for the children's to spend a glorious Christmas with them. Above and transcending all the Christmas carols will be the song of my heart: "Come, Lord Jesus" (Rev. 22:20); and in the curious continuum of time, I shall be simultaneously praying: Thanks be to God, He has come. He is coming again at Christmas, and He is yet to come with power and great glory (Mt. 24:30).

Just now my heart echoes the words of Saint Leo, "By the path of love whereby Christ came down to us, may we mount up to Him."

Jesus, I love You who have humbled yourself to be born in a manger. In total humility I prostrate myself before You who are at once a helpless Infant and the King of Kings. Lord of my life, as You have come down to me, lift me now to You.

In a few days we will be praying, "O God, you have caused this holy night to shine with the brightness of the true Light" (BCP, p. 212). Thanks be to God, that Light continues to shine on in the darkness, a darkness which can never overcome it (Jn. 1:5).

Come, O Come, Emmanuel. . . .

Epilogue

On January 31, 1978, I was ordained to the diaconate of the Episcopal Church, by the Right Reverend Robert B. Appleyard, D.D., Bishop of the Episcopal Diocese of Pittsburgh. The ordination took place in Pittsburgh (where I am still canonically resident) at Trinity Cathedral.

Bishop Appleyard honored me by preaching the ordination sermon. In it he remarked that I had been "spiritually" a deacon for years. This is true in that my calling has been, from the beginning, only to serve.

Many have asked me why I wanted to take this step. Among other reasons, it was to express my response to Him through the indelible sacrament of ordination: a "Yes" to the Lord, forever; an "official" promise to Him and to His Church, to serve Him always in this world and the next.

The Episcopal Church ordains three orders of clergy: bishops, priests, and deacons. From the early Middle Ages until this century, the diaconate has served merely as a stepping-stone to the priesthood. It is now being revived as a distinctive ministry as it was in the ancient Church (Acts 6) and actually is a far older ministry than the priesthood. The diaconate, as a separate and permanent order, recalls to the body of Christ, that our Lord came to serve and that the Church has a servant identity.

Ordained deacons personify, sacramentalize, and enable that ministry of service to which all Christians are called. Thus, as an historic, ordained ministry, it centers upon a ministry of service combined with a Gospel ministry (preaching and teaching) and a liturgical ministry (deaconing at the altar, preparing the oblations, reading the Gospel, coordinating the Great Intercession and proclaiming the Dismissal, as well as helping to administer the sacrament in church and taking the sacrament to the sick).[1]

After receiving my bishop's approval for ordination, I got in touch with all the Anglo-Catholic bishops and priests I knew, to ascertain their feeling about women in the diaconate. *I* felt that God had called me, but I have been known to misread the Holy Spirit, and I had no wish to add to the Church's controversy over the role of women. Without exception, all were in favor of women as deacons whether or not they approved of women priests. At the same time, I sought the permission of the Mother Superior of this community. She graciously extended it to me, with the understanding that I would not seek, nor expect, to serve as deacon at the convent. This I entirely understood and was more than willing to confine my service as deacon to Saint Thomas, where it was acceptable to the rector. However, the community has become more liberal, and to my great joy I am now permitted to serve as deacon here.

From the first, serving liturgically as deacon has been a source of indescribable joy and continuing wonder. Each and every time I find myself at the altar, I am awestruck and recall the words of Thomas Merton: "The altar is the living Christ and the linens are the members of His Mystical Body. Bringing their gifts to unite them with Him on the cross, I am dressing Christ in His members and clothing His sacrifice in the glory of a saved Church."[2]

Planning for the ordination was somewhat like planning a wedding. First came the setting of the date. It was no small task to find a time when the bishop was free and when I was between missions. Finally the date was set, and happily it turned out to be the feast day of Saint Marcella, a fourth-century saint of whom I had never heard, but with whom I immediately felt a sense of rapport when I learned that she was noted for her orthodoxy! Then, the invitations mailed, I nearly missed my own ordination.

I was on mission two weeks before the big event. On the second night, after the healing service, someone inadvertently slammed the heavy, outside door of the sacristy on one of my fingers, nearly amputating it. While someone called an orthopedic surgeon, the rector of the church rushed me to the hospital where the necessary surgery was performed. The priest remained at the hospital until early morning when I was wheeled out of the operating room. He claims that when I came to and looked at my hand with its colossal bandage, I exclaimed (I have no recollection of this): "How on earth can I be ordained with a hand like this?"

He called my bishop, who called me at the hospital a few hours later and said, "Don't worry about the ordination. It will proceed even if you have to be carried in to the cathedral on a stretcher!"

When I was released from the hospital three days later, I was told that I must remain at the rectory (the poor rector and his wife!) for at least five additional days before I could travel. Thanks be to God, I got to Pittsburgh in time, a bit battered but at least with a considerably smaller bandage!

The ordination. The closest to heaven I shall come on this earth. The great procession of clergy, those priests whom, for so long, I have deeply loved; those who presented me to the bishop on behalf of the clergy and people of the diocese of Pittsburgh; the much-loved chaplain from the convent, who sang the litany; my beloved friends, the rector from Saint Thomas and one of the women from there who has done so much to further the healing ministry; the priests who came from far distances in terrible weather, including the Roman Catholic priest who drove up from Washington, D.C., over icy roads; the beautiful music; the presence of my children who had come to share it all with me. Finally, as if in a dream, I stood before my bishop for the Examination: "My sister, do you believe that you are truly called by God and his Church to the life and work of a deacon?" "I believe I am so called." "May the Lord by his grace uphold you in the service he lays upon you." "Amen" (BCP, pp. 543–44).

Now, at long last, the Consecration. Kneeling before the bishop, his hands upon my head, I hear the prayer as if from afar off, "Therefore, Father, through Jesus Christ your Son, give your Holy Spirit to Emily; fill her with grace and power, and make her a deacon in your Church" (BCP, p. 545).

It was the most momentous and joyous day of my life. It was another wedding day, this time to my Lord.

Notes

PREFACE

1 Emily Gardiner Neal, *A Reporter Finds God* (Wilton, Conn.: Morehouse-Barlow, 1956).

2 The Commission chairman: the Right Reverend W. C. Campbell, Bishop of West Virginia, now retired.

CHAPTER 1: SPEAK, LORD. WHAT SHALL I DO?

1 *The Spiritual Exercises of St. Ignatius* (Garden City, N.Y.: Image Books, Doubleday, 1964), pp. 85 and 86.

CHAPTER 2: YOUR SERVANT HEARS. I GO.

1 Thomas Merton, *Praying the Psalms* (Collegeville, Minn.: Liturgical Press, 1956), p. 3.

CHAPTER 5: INNER HEALING

1 See, for example, Dennis and Matthew Linn, *Healing Life's Hurts* (New York: Paulist Press, 1978).

CHAPTER 6: APPOINTMENT WITH GOD

1 Saint John of The Cross, *Living Flame of Love* (Garden City, N.Y.: Image Books, Doubleday), stanza 111.

2 One such plan, among many, is The Bible Reading Fellowship, P.O. Box M, Winter Park, Fla. 32790.

3 Dom John Chapman, O.S.B., *Spiritual Letters* (London: Sheed and Ward, 1946), p. 99.

4 Among many: *Prayers New and Old* (Cincinnati: Forward Movement Publications, 1981; first published in 1937).

5 Thomas Whelan, *Benjamin* (New York: Newman Press, 1972), pp. 3-4.

CHAPTER 7: CELEBRATING LENT

1 Edward Poteat, "Stigmata," in *Masterpieces of Religious Verse*, ed. James Morrison (New York and London: Harper and Bros., 1948).

2 *Spiritual Counsel and Letters of Baron Friedrich von Hugel*, edited by Douglas Steere (New York: Harper and Row, 1964), pp. 24–25.

CHAPTER 8: "ACCORDING TO YOUR WORD"

1 Emily Gardiner Neal, *The Healing Power of Christ* (New York: Hawthorne Books, 1972), p. 44

2 Thomas Merton, *The Sign of Jonas* (Garden City, N.Y.: Image Books, Doubleday, 1956), p. 201.

CHAPTER 9: LIFE AFTER DEATH

1 See especially Raymond Moody, Jr., M.D., *Life After Life* (New York: Bantam Books, 1975).

2 Thomas Merton, *The Sign of Jonas*, p. 177.

CHAPTER 13: THE BREAD OF LIFE

1 Pope John XXIII, *Journal of a Soul* (New York: McGraw-Hill, 1965), p. 147.

2 Gregory Dix, *The Shape of the Liturgy* (London: Dacre Press, A. and C. Black, 1945), p. 161.

3 Ibid., p. 29.

4 Henri Nouwen, from an address at the National Conference of Trinity Institute, 2 February, 1981.

5 Ibid.

6 Simon Tugwell, *The Beatitudes: Soundings in Christian Traditions* (Springfield, Ill.: Templegate, 1980), p. 53.

CHAPTER 14: "TRUST IN HIM AND HE WILL ACT"

1 *Lesser Feasts and Fasts* (New York: Church Hymnal Corporation, 1980), p. 257.

CHAPTER 15: SALVATION, HEALING, AND THE LOVE OF GOD

1 *Lesser Feasts and Fasts*, p. 267.

CHAPTER 19: OUR BELOVED ALIVE

1 Emily Gardiner Neal, *In the Midst of Life* (Wilton, Conn.: Morehouse-Barlow, 1963).

CHAPTER 20: BE EXPECTANT

1 Shirley Hughson, O.H.C., *With Christ in God* (London: S.P.C.K., 1948), p. 237.

2 Thomas Merton, *New Seeds of Contemplation* (New York: New Directions, 1972), p. 35.

3 Ibid., p. 36.

CHAPTER 21: THE DOCTORS' MISSION

1 C. S. Lewis in a letter to Sheldon Vanauken; quoted in Sheldon Vanauken, *A. Severe Mercy* (New York: Harper and Row, 1977), p. 209.

CHAPTER 22: "MY LORD AND MY GOD!"

1 Taken from *The Little Chronicle*, vol. 57, no. 3 (December 1975).

2 Adrian van Kaam, *Spirituality and the Gentle Life* (Denville, N.J.: Dimension Books, 1974), p. 184.

3 Polish Christmas carol; quoted in Karol Wojtyla, *Sign of Contradiction* (New York: Seabury, 1979), p. 39.

EPILOGUE

1 Explanation of the diaconate is from *The Deacon in the Episcopal Church*, by the Rev. James L. Lowery, Jr. (Boston: National Center for the Diaconate).

2 Thomas Merton, *The Sign of Jonas*, p. 140.